THE
PLAN
AND THE
AGE OF THE
UNIVERSE

Volume VIII
Creation Science Series

By Dennis Gordon Lindsay

Published by
Christ For The Nations, Inc.
P.O. Box 769000
Dallas, Texas 75376-9000

Printed 1993
Copyright ©1993 by
Christ For The Nations, Inc.

All scripture NIV unless otherwise noted.

FOREWORD

The purpose of each volume of the Creation Science Series is to make information available to all laypersons interested in the subject. My intent is to provide uncomplicated documentation on the subject of Creation Science that is easy to read and comprehend, while leaving out much of the technical jargon that only a specialist would appreciate.

For those who desire additional information by professionals in the Creation Science community, the following outstanding organizations may be contacted:

MASTER BOOKS
9260 Isaac St., Suite E
Santee, CA 92071 USA

INSTITUTE FOR CREATION RESEARCH
2100 Greenfield Dr.
Box 2667
El Cajon, CA 92021 USA

BIBLE — SCIENCE ASSOCIATION
P.O. Box 32457
Minneapolis, MN 55432 USA

CREATION RESOURCE FOUNDATION
Box 570
El Dorado, CA 95623 USA

CREATION EVIDENCES MUSEUM
Box 309
Glen Rose, TX 76043 USA

Cover design by Don Day.
Illustrations by Diana Sisco and Camille Barnes.

TABLE OF CONTENTS

PART VI: THE END OF TIME AND THE COMING OF THE BIG BANG

Introduction

Questions, Questions, Questions.

How old is the Earth? What is the age of the universe? Is the Earth billions of years old? Isn't it a bit absurd that some Christians suggest the Bible claims that creation took place only about 6,000 years ago? Are there really scores of ways to show that the Earth and the universe are very young? Don't carbon-14 dating and other types of radioactive dating methods prove that the Earth is billions of years old? What is radiometric dating? Doesn't light coming from distant stars prove that the universe is far older than 6,000 years? Is the speed of light slowing down? Weren't rocks which the American astronauts brought back from the moon billions of years old, as was reported by the media and in scientific journals? How did the Apollo 11 moon landing baffle the evolutionists concerning the age of the moon?

How is it that live penguins, seals and mollusks have been dated as having been dead thousands of years? How did a California whale found on its tail give support for the concept of a young Earth? How do the basement rocks of the Earth discredit the theory of an ancient Earth? How do evolutionists use circular reasoning in their attempts to prove the age of fossils as millions of years? Where are all the multitudes of people that should be here if man has been walking on the Earth for a million years?

These and other questions will be answered in this volume and in the following volume of the Creation Science Series, which addresses the dating of fossils, rocks and bones. This volume will focus on the evidences which testify for a young creation while Volume IX, entitled *The Dismantling of Evolutionism's Sacred Cow*, zeroes in on the fallacies of radiometric dating. This volume will include 30 clocks which indicate creation is a recent event. They are as follows:

CLOCK	AGE INDICATOR
1. A Whale on its tale	Formation occurred suddenly
2. Lunar Dust	6,000 years
3. Lunar mountain erosion	Several thousands of years
4. Solar Sweeper	10,000 years maximum
5. The shrinking sun	1 million years maximum
6. The bulging Earth	500,000 years maximum
7. The receding moon	1 million years maximum
8. The magnetic Earth	10,000 years maximum
9. The Earth's core	10,000 years maximum
10. The oceans' elements:	
a. 29 elements	10,000 years or less
b. 8 elements	100,000 years or less
11. Coral formations	5,000 years
12. River deltas	4,500 years
13. Ocean sediments	100,000 years maximum
14. Niagara Falls	5,000 years
15. Mountain erosion	14 million years maximum
16. Soil production	10,000 years
17. Oil pressure	10,000 years maximum
18. Meteorite matter	A few thousand years
19. The redwoods	5,000 years
20. Cave formations	A few thousand years
21. Radiohalos	Instant creation
22. Comets	10,000 years maximum
23. Hot planets	A few thousand years
24. Saturn's rings	A few thousand years
25. Hot ringed planets	A few thousand years
26. Hot stars	A few thousand years max.
27. Sirius B	A few thousand years
28. Galaxy clusters	2-4 million years
29. M.I.T. and evolutionism	10 billion years not enough
30. Population statistics	5,000 years

PART I

HOW OLD IS THE EARTH?

Chapter One

Does It Really Matter?

Why are the birth of the Earth and the age of the universe so important? Aren't the issues of alcoholism, AIDS, abortion, drug addiction, pornography, crime and divorce far more significant?

Certainly society today has grave problems. What few people recognize, however, is that these problems are the evil outgrowth of the diabolical lies which society has been brainwashed to believe. We have been spoon-fed the lie that man is a product of millions of years of a slow and gradual process called evolution. It sounds so reasonable and has been taught by such reputable and educated men that many believe it must be the truth. However, this lie has destroyed the foundation of God's Word in our society and has opened the door for every kind of evil.

Evolutionists claim that death and decay existed billions of years before man ever set foot on this planet. This volume will expose the myth of an ancient Earth and explain why Satan has so unrelentlessly seen to it that this lie be propagated. If the Earth were billions of years old as evolutionists claim, then the Gospel of Jesus Christ would be of no value. For the Good News is that Jesus came to restore the broken relationship between God and man by dying for man's sin. According to Romans 5:12, it was the fall of man which brought about physical death and decay to all life on this planet. The record of fossils found buried deep within the layers of the Earth gives testimony to death, decay and struggle.

If each layer of the Earth represents millions of years, then Jesus came to the wrong planet and His mission was a mistake. Death, then, was not a result of sin, but simply a result of natural selection — a slow and gradual process which supposedly directs evolution to occur.

If physical death was not a result of man's sin as scripture states, then there is no need to repent, no need for a Savior. The Bible contains error and therefore cannot be trusted. The Atonement — Christ dying to restore all creation including the broken relationship between man and his Creator — is nothing more than a nice religious myth.

Can you see the importance of the creation issue? That is why this volume is dedicated to revealing the overwhelming evidence in favor of a very young creation. This study will also enhance the readers' understanding of the amazing supernatural power of a living God Who rules and reigns over His creation, yesterday, today and forever.

Chapter Two

Testimony 1: A Tale of a Balancing Whale on Its Tail

Diatoms — Microscopic Sea Creatures.

One of the most intriguing discoveries of a fossil was made in a rock quarry in Southern California. The discovery proved to be an exceptional challenge to the evolutionary belief that each layer of sedimentary rock was formed slowly and gradually over an immense period of time. **(See fig. 1.)**

The rock quarry in question is composed of the shells of microscopic sea creatures known as diatoms. **(See fig. 2.)** Diatoms are extremely tiny plants which live in the oceans. They are about one-fourth the thickness of a human hair. These marvels of architectural engineering are found in three dimensions in all known geometrical shapes — circles, stars, squares, triangles and

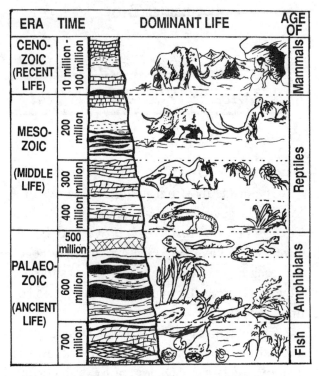

Figure 1. MYTHOLOGICAL EVOLUTIONARY CHART
OF GEOLOGICAL DIVISIONS OF TIME

ovals. The intricate design and engineering of
these creatures are evidence of intelligence in
their origin. The shells are designed with such
remarkable symmetric detail that they are used
to check the precision and quality of optic lenses

Figure 2. DIATOMS: A FANTASY FROM INNER SPACE

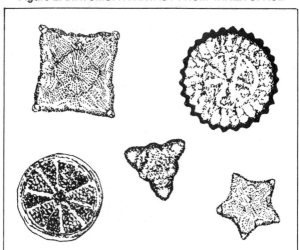

manufactured for microscopes. Also, the white chalky deposits comprised of the shells of these tiny creatures are mined and used commercially for fertilizer, insulation for soundproofing materials and detergent for swimming pool filters.

When diatoms die, their shells do not decompose. Instead, they gradually settle down to the ocean floor. Under certain appropriate conditions they form deposits called diatomaceous Earth. These deposits can be hundreds of feet in thickness and be remarkably free of contaminants. Evolutionism asserts that these deposits have been formed gradually over millions of years. The shells are so tiny that evolutionists have assumed that it would require a vast amount of time to form a layer just one foot deep. Such reasoning is based on present-day conditions for the formation of such a deposit.

Remarkable Discovery.

Recently, it has been discovered that diatom deposits can form in a relatively short period of time. At the quarry in Lompoc, California, during mining operations in 1976, workers came upon the fossil remains of the skeleton of a baleen whale. What is so unusual is that the whale fossil is standing on its tail in the quarry. **(See fig. 3.)** It is gradually being exposed as the diatomite rock is mined. The fossil is about eighty feet long.

What does this find mean? In a nutshell, it indicates that this formation could not have built up gradually over thousands of years as evolutionists have assumed. The billions of tiny diatomite shells making up the formation had to have been deposited in a very short period of time. For one thing, when a whale (or any creature) dies, it does not, under normal conditions, become a fossil. Secondly, whales

Figure 3. A WHALE OF A TALE

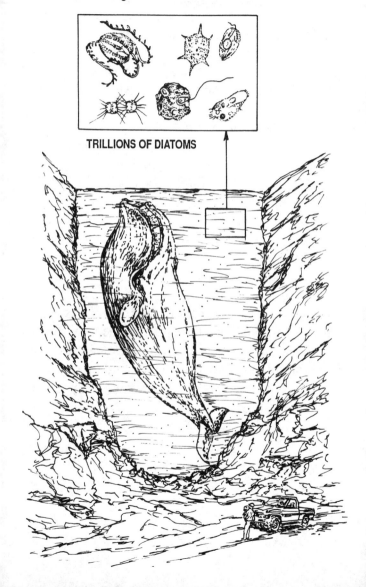

TRILLIONS OF DIATOMS

don't stand on their tails — alive or dead! The whale had to have been buried deeply and quickly in wet sediment to seal it off from the atmosphere, bacteria and so forth. Otherwise it would have simply rotted and the skeleton would have decomposed and turned into dust.

Testimony for a Young Earth.

Obviously, the eighty-foot-long whale did not remain on its tail so that billions of tiny diatoms could gradually cover it up. The formation containing the whale had to be deposited quickly in order for the whale not to rot, decompose and turn to dust, bones and all.

The whale on its tail is just one of many examples in the universe which testify to a young Earth. It also stands as evidence of the Genesis Flood, which caused catastrophic conditions that quickly formed vast layers of sedimentary rock while at the same time entombing creatures by the millions — like this whale found on its tail. This is only one of many testimonies to a young Earth.

Chapter Three

The Birth of Planet Earth

Figure 4. HOW OLD IS THE EARTH?

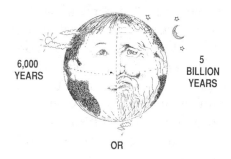

6,000
YEARS

5
BILLION
YEARS

OR

How Old is the Earth?

The most direct answer is that no one really knows. There is no scientific means by which one can measure accurately the age of the Earth or of the universe. However, there are various geological evidences which give us clues as to the Earth's age.

Evolutionary Fallacy.

Evolutionists give the impression that they can accurately date various rock formations which they claim go back hundreds of millions of years. Many evolutionary science books emphatically state that the beginning of our solar system, with its sun and nine planets, took place some 4½ billion years ago, and the beginning of the universe 10-20 billion years ago. A few evolutionists would now like to push the origin of the universe back to 30 billion years. However, the truth of the matter is that these time measurements are all made on the basis of assumptions which cannot be proven or tested. The immense ages assigned to rocks and fossils by evolutionists are nothing more than a wishful guess. Furthermore, these measurements are in direct violation to some of the most basic laws of physics, such as the first and second laws of thermodynamics.[1]

Isn't there any scientific evidence that the Earth is billions of years old? If you were to ask the average person on the street this question, he or she would answer unhesitatingly, "Yes!" However, if his life depended on coming up with one positive proof, he would be unable to do so.

The reason there is such a worldwide belief that there is evidence for the evolutionary theory is the result of indoctrinization by evolutionary

---

[1] The first and second laws of thermodynamics are discussed in Volume II of the Creation Science Series entitled *The Harmony of Science and Scripture*.

scientists. They claim a lot of things about the theory of evolutionism that simply are not fact.

Though the public assumes that the evolutionary community has firmly established the age of the Earth, the truth is that they have not, and the more candid evolutionists will admit it. For example, evolutionist Dr. Stephen Moorebath of the University of Oxford, stated:

> No terrestrial rocks closely approaching an age of 4.6 billion years have yet been discovered. The evidence for the age of the earth is circumstantial, being based upon ... indirect reasoning (*Scientific American*, March 1977, p. 92).

Another evolutionist, Dr. John Eddy of the High Altitude Observatory in Boulder, Colorado, stated in the prestigious journal *Geotimes:*

> There is no evidence based solely on solar observations that the sun is 4½ to 5 billion years old ... I suspect that the sun is 4½ billion years old. However, given some new and unexpected results to the contrary, and some time for frantic recalculation and theoretical readjustment, I suspect that we

could live with Bishop Ussher's value
for the age of the Earth and Sun. I don't
think we have much in the way of
observational evidence in astronomy
to conflict with that. (*Geotimes*, Sept.
1978, p. 18).

Did you get that? There is *no evidence* that
the sun is 4½ billion years old and Bishop
Ussher's age for the Earth and sun may be closer
to the truth than it has been thought. Bishop
Ussher believes the Earth is about 6,000 years
old. How is it possible that an evolutionary astronomer would concede that there is really no
scientific evidence that is inconsistent with a
6,000-year-old Earth? Is he fed up with the glar-
ing inconsistencies and obvious contradictions
of the evolutionary faith? Whatever the reason,
it is apparent that there is no conclusive evidence
for an ancient Earth. As Dr. Donald Chittick
points out: "The idea that the Earth is very, very
old is not in any way suggested by any studies in
science. It arises as a result of rejecting Special
Creation."

So the next time someone begins to insist that
the Earth is billions of years old, ask them: "How
do you know that it is so old? Were you there?"
If they respond by claiming that there are dating

methods that prove the Earth is billions of years old, then ask if he could supply a list of some of them. If by chance he remembers one of the radiometric processes such as uranium-lead, then ask, "Are these methods of dating absolute or are there certain assumptions built into them which cannot be proven?" If he hasn't walked off, and if he is honest, he will have to concede that there is not one dating method which can positively establish a verifiable date for the Earth. (We will examine these dating assumptions in Volume IX of the Creation Science Series entitled *The Dismantling of Evolutionism's Sacred Cow: Radiometric Dating*.)

The Biblical Account.

Although conservative Bible scholars no longer strictly hold to Ussher's dating system, for the Christian the Bible is the final authority on any subject which it specifically addresses.

The Bible indicates that creation took place rather recently — around 6,000 years ago. In Genesis 5, we find a list of Adam's descendants and their ages.

> When Adam had lived 130 years, he had a son ... he named him Seth ... and had other sons and daughters (verses 3,4).

As we read on we find that when Seth was 105 years old, he had a son named Enosh, and the list of descendants goes on to the end of the chapter.

In Genesis 11, after Noah and his family had come out of the Ark, there is another list of names along with the age of each when his son was born. This list proceeds right up to Abraham, who lived about 4,000 years ago. If we go through these two lists and work out how many years there were from Adam to Abraham, we find that Adam was created between 6,000 and 7,000 years ago, which gives us a very good idea of the Earth's age. (See fig. 5.) If it seems preposterous to suggest that the Earth could be this young, remember that no one has ever proven that the Earth or universe is millions or billions of years old.

Occasionally one will argue that the Bible is not concerned with the "when" and "how" of creation, but rather it is only concerned with the "Who" and "why" of creation and its inhabitants. Such a statement immediately should sound an alarm in one's spirit because the individual who made the statement has little regard or under-standing for the authority of Scripture.

It is true that the Scriptures were not written to be a textbook on history or science. However, when the Word of God touches on any area, we must accept it as being inspired and without error.

The truth of the matter is, the Bible is a book that is grounded in history, and is utterly filled with chronological data. As Professor Edwin Thiele has pointed out:

> Chronology is important. Without chronology, it is not possible to understand history, for chronology is the backbone of history. We know that God regards chronology as important, for He has put so much of it into His Word. We find chronology not only in the historical books of the Bible, but also in the prophetic books, in the Gospels and in the writings of Paul. (Edwin Thiele, *A Chronology of the Hebrew Kings*, Grand Rapids, MI, Zondervan, 1975, p. 7)

Of course most Bible scholars are aware of the fact that the biblical genealogies do not always reflect a strict father-son relationship. Occasionally there are some gaps in the lineage records. The reason we know these gaps exist is that the missing names are supplied elsewhere in

Figure 5. ADAM TO ABRAHAM

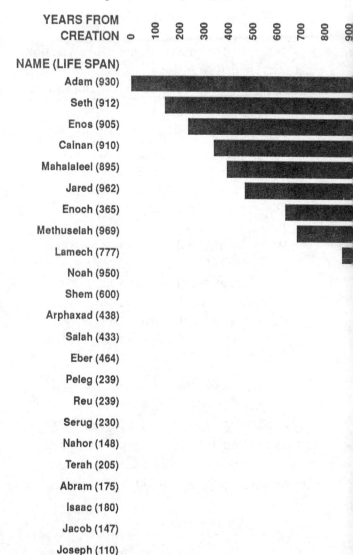

YEARS FROM CREATION

	0	100	200	300	400	500	600	700	800	900

NAME (LIFE SPAN)

Adam (930)
Seth (912)
Enos (905)
Cainan (910)
Mahalaleel (895)
Jared (962)
Enoch (365)
Methuselah (969)
Lamech (777)
Noah (950)
Shem (600)
Arphaxad (438)
Salah (433)
Eber (464)
Peleg (239)
Reu (239)
Serug (230)
Nahor (148)
Terah (205)
Abram (175)
Isaac (180)
Jacob (147)
Joseph (110)

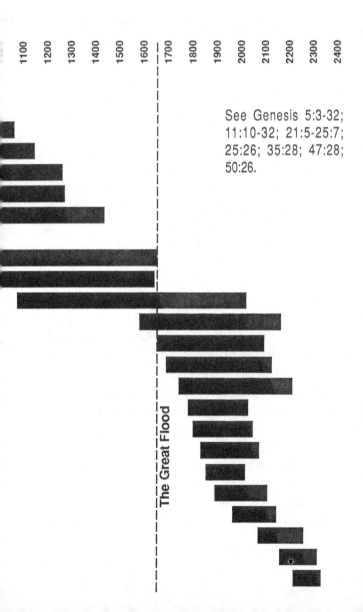

See Genesis 5:3-32;
11:10-32; 21:5-25:7;
25:26; 35:28; 47:28;
50:26.

The Great Flood

the Bible. But when the total biblical picture is
seen there really are no gaps.

When a Son Isn't a Father's Son.

Some Bible scholars contend for an
additional several thousand years to be added to
the 6,000 most creationists believe is the number
of years since creation. The reason for such
speculation arises because of the Hebrew word
translated to English as *begat*. In the Hebrew,
begat does not have the same meaning as it does
in English; it does not necessarily mean a father
and son relationship, but sometimes refers to an
ancestral relationship. It can refer to a
grandfather or great-grandfather or even a
slightly wider separation. It is for this reason that
some genealogies, when compared to others,
leave out one or two individuals. It is possible
that several additional generations could be
squeezed into the 10 generations from Adam to
Noah. However, the idea that a great number of
generations could fit in cannot be supported by
scripture. There is so much genealogical material
in scripture, that cross-checking can reveal a
complete genealogy in almost every case.

Difficulties also arise from dates in the Bible
which refer to kings and their length of reign.
Sometimes there is an overlap of time. But this

can easily be explained. When a son of a king came to the throne, his reign overlapped his father's in some cases. The king was still alive, but had turned over the daily responsibilities to his son.

There is only a slight variation in dates given in scripture. Even adding them all in, the age of the Earth is a maximum of 10,000 years. This, of course, is a far cry from the billions of years suggested by evolutionism.[2]

Scriptural Evidence for a Young World.

The following points are a summary of the biblical doctrine of a young creation:

1. God spoke the following words directly to Moses: "For in six days the LORD made the heavens and the earth, the sea, and all that is in them" (Ex. 20:11).

2. Genesis 1 specifically says that each of the six days of creation consisted of one evening and one morning. For example: "And there was evening, and there was morning — the fifth day" (Gen. 1:23).

3. Adam and Eve were created on the sixth day (Gen. 1:27). The time from the sixth day of

---

2 The possibility of an enormous gap of time between the beginning of creation (Gen. 1:1) and the time when God formed Adam (Gen. 1:26) from the dust of the Earth has been proposed by some theologians and is known as the Gap Theory and the Day Age Theory. These theories have no scriptural basis nor any scientific foundation. Such theories were created to accommodate evolutionism. A thorough explanation of the fallacies and errors associated with each theory will be covered in a subsequent volume of the Creation Science Series.

creation until Adam's death was 930 years. The creation days each consisted of one morning and evening, and Adam lived through at least part of the sixth day plus the entire seventh day and all the additional days of 930 years.

4. Exodus 20:11 confirms that God created all that is in heaven and earth in six days.

Ancient Written Records.

In addition to the biblical account for a recent creation, the 22nd edition of Robert Young's concordance lists 37 ancient written records, all of which place the date of creation no earlier than 7,000 B.C.

If you were applying for a driver's license and were asked to provide proof of your age, you couldn't use your own word or the word of a friend, or your parents' word — even if you appeared to be 30 years of age. The only valid way would be to provide identification such as your birth certificate. In other words, the only way to accurately determine your precise age is by means of a written record. Likewise, the only valid means we have for determining the age of ancient civilizations is by means of the written records they left behind.

When evolutionists insist that man has been roaming the Earth for the past three million years, and that ancient civilizations can be updated to 50,000 years B.C., they are speculating. And if you keep up with the *National Geographic* reports on new finds, such dates, like airline schedules, are subject to change at a moment's notice. All of those dates are based on radiometric dating methods, which are highly unreliable beyond a few thousand years. The earliest civilizations known to man are those which have left records — such as the ancient Sumerian nation of Mesopotamia, which goes back to about 3,500 B.C. These are the only absolute records for dating early man.

Human history and Earth history started at the same time. Human history can only be measured in terms of several thousand years, and therefore Earth history is likewise limited to a few thousand years. This being the case, it is impossible for evolutionism to have occurred.

The Heart of the Issue.

It must be understood right from the beginning of our discussion that with the evolutionist the issue is not a matter of time but it is about the *Creator*. The question is not whether the Earth is ancient, but whether there can be an Ancient of Days in our discussion at all. Once the Creator of Time enters the discussion, the skeptic becomes uncomfortable and feels the urge to exit. No one likes heart surgery, and God has a way of exposing wicked hearts. For anyone who rejects God, the only alternative is to accept a naturalistic, materialistic explanation for the origin of life.

A devoted evolutionist cannot be open-minded on the question of a young Earth because the theory of evolution requires vast amounts of time. Thus for evolutionists, the question has never been "How old is the Earth and universe?" but "*How* are the universe and Earth old?" They have already decided that the Earth must be extremely old; that is the only way that evolutionism supposedly can work. Therefore, the question of a young Earth is non-negotiable. There is absolutely no place for God in the humanist's heart, for he desires to sit on the throne — he alone.

The Doctrine of Mature Creation.

If one accepts the Genesis account as historically true, then Adam and Eve must be regarded as sudden and "mature" creations. And they lived in a "mature" world. In other words, from the moment of their creation, they were fully developed and mature in every respect. Such a concept is based on the biblical principle and doctrine of an instant and mature creation. This view will be fully explained in section two of this volume.

Chapter Four

Geochronology

Figure 6. GRANDFATHER TIME

Timekeepers.

Throughout history man has found ways of knowing the time of the day and of the year. Clocks can be found on city towers, cars, computers, calculators, checkbooks, coffee-makers, radios, rings, submarines — or just about anywhere. Nature also has provided many natural clocks which provide man with ways of telling the time of day, the time of year and even the ages of the Earth, moon, sun and the universe.

Geochronology is the science of determining the age of the Earth by geological events. *Geo* means Earth and *chronology* has to do with a time sequence. Scientists are aware of over 80 ways nature indicates the Earth's age. These are called "geologic clocks." These clocks are based on natural processes that are presently occurring and can be measured.

An example of one such natural process would be the formation of diatomaceous Earth which was previously mentioned. Another example would be the rate dust is falling to the Earth (illustrated in the following chapter). The majority of "geologic clocks" give a relatively young age for the Earth. Only a few of them yield a preliminary conclusion of billions of years; those which do are based on evolutionary assumptions which cannot be verified.

Certain variables can throw off the accuracy of a clock. A worldwide flood, for instance, would have speeded up a clock causing something very young to appear to be very old. (Remember the diatomaceous rock with the whale found on its tail. The formation of other geological wonders such as the Grand Canyon also are examples.)

In the past, when many scientists believed that evolutionism was indisputably true, it seemed there was no choice but to accept the ages espoused by that theory. Since evolutionists "knew" the Earth was old, clocks were interpreted accordingly. But, as we have learned more and more about nature's clocks, their testimony has grown more inconsistent. It has become clear that there is something drastically wrong with the evolutionary claims of an ancient universe. Nature's clocks attest to a young Earth and universe.

Chapter Five

Testimony 2: The Case of the Missing Dust

Praise the Lord for Dust!

We despise dust, mostly because we have to go to so much trouble to rid our homes of it. But God created it for a purpose. He weighed it out in His balances for an orderly creation (Isa. 40:15). Without it, our planet could not have the life-giving rain, the blue sky, the beautiful sunsets and dawns.

Dust also serves mankind in another important way; it is a vital clock in nature that helps to tell the age of our planet. Just as the dust on a coffee table can tell us about how long it has been since it was last dusted, the dust on the Earth tells us something about its age.

Evolutionism's Dusty Burial.

As previously mentioned, evolutionism proposes that our solar system is somewhere in

Figure 7. MISSION TO THE MOON

©CB 1993

the neighborhood of 4½ billion years old. Creationists believe the solar system to be only about 6,000 years old. The enormous difference between these two proposals boggles the mind.

There are many clocks in nature that suggest the age of our planetary system, and one involves dust. The age of our planet can be determined by measuring the amount of cosmic dust which accumulates on it.

Let us travel out into space and consider some dust that literally buries the evolutionary concept of an ancient solar system. Scientists know that outer space contains an abundance of tiny specks of material known as cosmic dust. This cosmic dust is constantly falling into our atmosphere, collecting on the Earth's surface and mixing with all sorts of other material by the action of wind and water. This cosmic dust collects on all sizable space bodies, such as the moon and other planets. (See fig. 8.)

Meteoric dust consists of particles so tiny, and moving so slowly through space that they fail to generate the friction heat necessary to burn up upon entering the atmosphere. Instead they settle gently to Earth's surface, and come to rest, along with regular dust particles. Scientists have collected dust in chemical trays and analyzed it to determine how much of it is extra-terrestrial

Figure 8. DUSTY OL' MAN MOON

©CB 1993

in origin. The amount of dust that falls each day is then used to calculate how much falls each year.

Extraterrestrial Food.

Scientists tell us that 20,000 tons of cosmic dust fall on planet Earth each year — or about 50 tons a day. This means there is some on everyone's head and in everyone's stomach. Most of it is microscopic in size. If the Earth is 4½ billion years old, there should be a lot of cosmic dust on the Earth. Here is the question: Where is the dust? Harold Slusher, Director of the Kidd Memorial Seismological Observatory and Assistant Professor of Geophysics at the University of Texas at El Paso, points out that the influx of meteoric dust into the Earth's atmosphere indicates the planet is only a few thousand years old.

Before man set foot on the moon, some scientists argued that there did not appear to be enough cosmic dust in the surface layers of the Earth to account for the supposed billions of years of Earth's history. However, evolutionists argued that extensive wind and water erosion have hidden the dust and that it had been either buried in the layers of the Earth or washed into the oceans and become part of the deep sediment layers of the ocean's floor. If this were true, the oceans should contain a tremendous amount of nickel, since nickel forms a considerable part of most meteorites. However, the amount of this element found in sea water indicates an accumulation of only a few thousand years, rather than billions! Evolutionists insisted that the missing cosmic dust would turn up somewhere. But investigation has failed to locate — either on land or in the oceans — the significantly large amounts of cosmic dust that would back up their theory.

Figure 9. MARTIAN MOON MINING, INC.

Mining Moon Dust.

With their knowledge of the annual rate of cosmic dust accumulation, scientists have estimated the amount of cosmic dust that would have settled on the surface of the moon over time. On the moon there is no environment to cause erosion like we have on Earth. One must assume that "in the beginning" the moon's surface was free of any cosmic dust. One must also suppose that cosmic dust has been settling on its surface throughout its history at the same rate as it does today. And finally, one must expect that no unknown factors have interfered with the constant accumulation of the dust.[3] Then one has a good basis for a simple clock to estimate the age of the moon. Such a calculation would help to establish the age of the Earth as well as the other planets in our solar system, since all are considered to be of the same age.

Space Probes Can't Find the Dust.

Because on the moon there is no erosion to wash or blow dust away, it becomes deeper and deeper. Since evolutionists were convinced that the moon was at least 4.5 billion years old, the idea of a slow but steady fall of space dust caused some concern. The space scientists worried about the dangers of making a soft landing on the moon. On the basis of annual measurements of cosmic dust landing on the Earth,

---

[3] e.g., Some extraterrestrial mining industry which at some time in the past has removed much of the dust for commercial purposes. As ridiculous as this may sound, it must be remembered that the U.S. government is spending billions of dollars in search of life beyond our Earth.

evolutionary scientists calculated that a very conservative estimation would be 50-180 feet of loosely packed cosmic dust on the moon's surface. Some estimated the dust might be as much as two miles deep. The great fear was that when the lunar lander fired its retro-rockets in order to soft land, the astronauts would be buried by the blast of dust and would never be able to take off for the return trip to Earth. (See fig. 10.)

As a result of the scientists' concern, unmanned probes were sent to the moon to evaluate the conditions of the surface before man began his journey there. The vast amounts of expected dust were not found by the probes. Theories were numerous as to its whereabouts; maybe it had collected in *unknown* areas from *unknown* disturbances.

As blast-off time approached for the first moon landing, there was not only intense excitement, but considerable apprehension as to what might be found there, particularly over the moon-dust problem. Many precautions were taken. Additional expensive impact probes were sent to check for safe landing sites. Scientists believed it crucial to include huge saucer-like landing pods in the design of the lunar lander. These were attached to the legs of the lunar lander so that it would safely settle down without sinking into the theorized dust layer. (See fig. 11.)

Figure 10. THE DISAPPEARING ACT

Figure 11. THE POINTLESS PODS

Touchdown: July 20, 1969.

Finally the great day came; the space rocket roared into orbit and then out into the heavens. It traveled thousands of miles, finally reaching the moon, where the lander was detached. Millions of Earthlings watched via TV, holding their breath as the Eagle slowly descended to the surface. I can still recall where I was and what I was doing at that very moment.

The moment of truth finally arrived. The spacecraft planted itself firmly on solid ground known as Mare Tranquillitatis. It didn't disappear into hundreds of feet of dust! Not long after the landing, Neil Armstrong became the first man to set foot on the moon. Many can still remember the immortalized words he spoke for all the world to hear: "One small step for man, and one giant leap for mankind." Since that time, most everyone has read or heard those words as they have been replayed hundreds of times by the media. But most likely no one can recall the conversation that surrounded those famous words as Armstrong communicated with NASA's mission control center. He spoke words that bury the evolutionary theory of an ancient solar system.

"Where's the Dust?"

Although astronaut Armstrong communicated in a matter-of-fact manner and technical lingo, in effect he was saying, "Where is all the dust?"

> The LH footpads are only depressed in
> the surface about 1 or 2 inches,
> although the surface appears to be
> very, very fine grained, as you get

close to it. It's almost like a powder. Down there, it's very fine. ... And the, the surface is fine and powdery. I can, I can pick it up loosely with my toe. It does adhere in fine layers like powdered charcoal to the sole and sides of my boots. I only go in a small fraction of an inch, maybe an eighth of an inch, but I can see the footprints of my boots and the treads in the fine, sandy particles.

Three times Armstrong repeats that there was very little dust. The entire conversation is available on transcript for anyone writing to NASA in Houston, Texas. These statements about the dust have been virtually ignored by the evolutionary community in their publications and TV documentaries. The reason is simple; no one wants to shoot his own foot. No one wants to talk about an overwhelming evidence that destroys the credibility of one's own belief system which requires the age of the Earth to be billions of years.

More Dust in the Face of Evolutionism.

To further substantiate that the moon dust was missing, and to the humiliation of evolutionism, there was a problem implanting the American Flag. Watch the early clips documenting that momentous occasion when man first walked on the moon; check out the difficulty Neil Armstrong encountered when he attempted to plant the American flag by hammering it down into the supposed billions of years of accumulated cosmic dust. Armstrong pounded, but the flag would not stand securely because the anticipated heavy dust layer simply was not there. There was a layer of dust, but it was only a couple of inches thick.

Testimony to a Young Earth.

The trip to the moon revealed that cosmic dust had only been falling for a few thousand years. There was just enough dust for footprints (1/8"-3"). **(See fig. 12.)**

This dusty moon clock in one second dissolved the imaginary billions of years that evolutionists have been proclaiming as the age of the Earth-moon system. It also devastated the Gap Theory and Day Age Theory to which some believers ascribe. Some Christian theologians and professors have become intimidated by the assertions of evolutionism. They have fallen prey to their influence and have attempted to

Figure 12. FAMOUS FOOTPRINTS

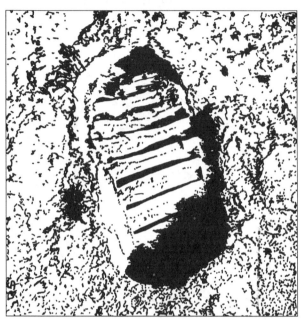

force the Scriptures to harmonize with the ancient Earth concept. The Gap Theory[4] is an attempt to marry evolutionism with the Bible by suggesting that there were two creations.

As bothersome as dust can be, this is one time it shines with an illustrious glow — pointing to a mighty and powerful Creator capable of

---

[4] The Gap Theory is covered in a subsequent volume of the Creation Science Series.

creating man out of the dust of the Earth, and breathing into him the breath of life (Gen. 2:7).

Chapter Six

Testimony 3: Anyone for a Hot Potato?

Figure 13. ANYONE FOR A HOT POTATO?

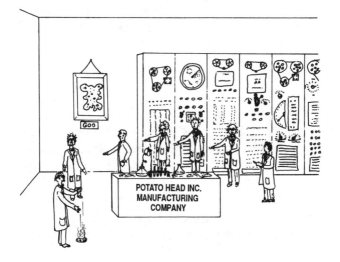

POTATO HEAD INC.
MANUFACTURING
COMPANY

Dropped Like a Hot Potato.

Overnight, the issue of moon dust disappeared out of sight as if it had been sucked into a black hole. The issue was dropped like a hot potato. In spite of evidence to the contrary, most evolutionists maintain their dogma of vast eons of time since the origin of the universe. Their only alternative would be to admit error. So instead of accepting the obvious, evolutionists continue to look for some other explanation for the small amount of dust on the moon.

Evolutionists have tried to skirt the moon dust issue by suggesting that prior to the Apollo moon mission, the majority of scientists didn't believe there would be much dust and that it was only a minority fringe group that thought otherwise. If this is true, then why was an extra one billion dollars spent (a conservative estimate) prior to the first Apollo moon mission because of concern about the dust problem? For example, as early as 1959, atheistic Isaac Asimov, a prolific writer, predicted that meteoritic dust upon the moon was at least 50 feet deep. (*Science Digest*, Jan. 1959, pp. 33-36).

The scientists' concern for the safety of the men is to be admired. Such a concern has its roots in the Word of God. On the other hand, there is little or no concern for human life (other than one's own) outside of the Bible. It is evident that humanists, atheists, pagan religions and evolutionists have no basis of concern for human life. That is why over 1.6 million babies are being slaughtered each year in abortuaries across the U.S. Such a holocaust is the result of the indoctrination of humanistic evolutionism.

The Truth of the Matter.

Some evolutionists have attempted to discredit the importance of the dust issue. But the truth of the matter is well documented in various publications. For example, *The Rand McNally New Concise Atlas of the Universe* (1978, pg. 41) states, "The theory that the Maria (Mare Tranquillitatis) was covered with deep layers of soft dust was current until well into the 1960s." Furthermore, once the astronauts were safely back on Earth, they were invited to be on Bob Hope's nationally-televised special. Hope asked Neil Armstrong what his greatest fear was before he set that first historic foot on the moon's surface. Without hesitation, Armstrong responded that his greatest fear was regarding the moon dust layer that scientists had told the astronauts to expect.

Additional Documentation.

The best source of documentation that evolutionists did in fact believe there was a deep layer of dust on the moon is found in textbooks. Evolutionists were much more candid before creationists began forcing the issue.

For example, we read in *Dynamic Astronomy*:

> The moon was for many years characterized as having a thick layer of dust covering its surface, into which an object would sink if it landed there.[5]

The $64,000 Question.

How do we account for such a small amount of moon dust if the moon is, in fact, several billion years old? We know the rate at which cosmic dust falls on the Earth and the yearly accumulation. If we assume the rate has not varied throughout time, as even the evolutionists maintain, then how do we account for an accumulation of only a couple of inches on the moon? This is the question, and it is yet to be answered logically and reasonably by evolutionists. The answer is quite simple. The moon and the Earth are not $4\frac{1}{2}$ billion years old; but rather, as the Bible reveals, less than 6,000 years.

Testimony 3: More Missing Mountains of Dust.

Scientists tell us that the mountains of the moon are eroding due to radiation from the sun and from outer space. This invisible radiation is striking the surface of the mountains, eroding

---

5 Dynamic Astronomy, Robert T. Dixon, 1971.

them. In the mid-1950's, R. A. Lyttleton, highly-respected astronomer and consultant to the U.S. Space program, wrote:

> The lunar surface is exposed to direct sunlight, and the strong ultra-violet light and X-rays can destroy the surface layers of exposed rocks and reduce them to dust at the rate of a few ten-thousandths of an inch per year. But even this minute amount could — during the age of the moon — be sufficient to form a layer over it several miles deep.[6]

Now a few ten-thousandths of an inch a year isn't much dust; but when you multiply even this infinitesimal amount by 4½ billion years, it amounts to 20-60 miles of dust — on top of the previously mentioned missing cosmic dust! If our astronauts had sunk into miles of dust on the moon, the evolutionists would have proclaimed this as "proof" of the great age of the moon. But they found only enough dust for footprints.

The silence of the evolutionists is strangely loud regarding the "disappearance" of the dust. No one likes dust thrown in his face, but the evolutionists have had cosmic dust blown in theirs.

---

6 Wysong, The Creation-Evolution Controversy, p. 387

Chapter Seven

Testimony 4: Solar Sweeper in the Sky

Figure 14. SOLAR SWEEPER

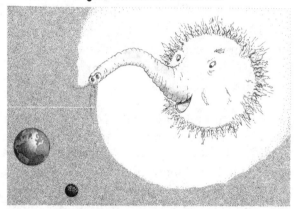

A Solar Sweeper Clock.

There is another kind of clock associated with our discussion of cosmic dust. It has to do with the dust particles in space which are being swept away by the sun's powerful gravity. The tiny cosmic dust particles, the same ones that settle on the moon, exist throughout the entire solar system. Our sun is vacuuming up these dust particles. Measuring the amount of time it is taking the sun to vacuum up the dust represents another type of natural clock by which we can estimate the age of the solar system.

To better understand how this clock works, think of a person who is employed by a professional janitorial cleaning service and is responsible for vacuuming a 20-story office building. By calculating the time it takes to vacuum the carpet on one floor, since all levels are exactly alike, we can determine approximately how long it will take him to complete the entire 20-story building. The amount of carpet that has been swept makes for a kind of clock that indicates how long the carpet cleaning person has been working at the job. The more carpet that has been swept, the more time has passed since the job began.

Now imagine a huge carpet the size of our solar system — our sun with all of its planets orbiting within it. The sun is the professional janitor in the solar system; it constantly "vacuums" the smaller particles of dust and debris. Its suction power is enormous. Astronomers tell us the sun is sweeping space with its powerful gravitational vacuum field at the rate of about 100,000 tons per day. The planets' gravitational fields also serve as solar sweepers.

At the present rate, the sun and the planets are vacuuming the dust in our solar system, most of it should have been removed in less than 15 million years. However, the average size and location of most of the particles of dust in the solar system indicate that they are less than 10,000 years in age.

From an evolutionary perspective of 4½ billion years for the age of our solar system, all particles up to three inches in diameter should have been swept into the sun up to the distance of Jupiter — unless some cosmic neighbor has been sweeping the dust out of his galactical home and distributing it throughout our solar system. Could this be where the missing moondust has gone? Maybe it was blown off the moon back into space during a "big sneeze" from the sun during one of its solar storms!

Seriously now, the Bible has the answer: Creation was a recent event — one that took place around 6,000 years ago.

PART II

THE DOCTRINE OF MATURE CREATION

Chapter Eight

Evolutionism's Most Persuasive Argument

Figure 15. THE ANDROMEDA GALAXY

Faster than a Speeding Bullet.

The Andromeda Galaxy is a large one composed of billions of stars. It is a galaxy similar to our own. It is two million light years away from Earth. **(See fig. 16.)**

When we look out into the universe, we are looking back in time. Thus, when we look towards the Andromeda Galaxy, we are not looking at it as it is today, but rather as it was in the past. At the present speed of light, it takes two million years for its light to arrive at our planet. If that is how long it takes light to travel, how could light coming from distant galaxies millions of light years away already have reached our planet if creation took place only about 6,000 years ago?

Over the years, the evolutionists' most persuasive argument for an ancient origin of the universe has been the speed of light. This argument is based on the present measured speed of light (186,000 miles per second) — the time it now takes light to travel. Some stars and galaxies are believed to be billions of light years from Earth. Could it be that scientists are mistaken about the immense size of the universe and the distance to the farthest known objects in the heavens? Even if they are mistaken, it is still difficult to believe that such remote stars are not more than 6,000 light years away.

According to the studies of some astronomers, light may take a "shortcut" as it travels in

Figure 16. LOOKING BACK IN TIME

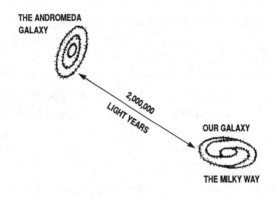

deep outer space. If their theory has validity, it suggests that it does not take light nearly as long to reach the Earth from outer space as is commonly believed. By the use of certain mathematical calculations, it is speculated that light could reach the Earth from the fartherest known star in about 15 years. (See Richard Niessen's "Starlight and the Age of the Universe," ICR *Impact,* July 1983.)

How then is it possible that the entire universe could be only a few thousand years old? Many evolutionists believe that the speed of light has scored a sound victory for them and that creation science has suffered a setback. However, this is far from the case. There is a solution to the dilemma which is simple and yet profound. When God created the universe, He created a fully developed, fully functional and mature universe — one which had a superficial appearance of age. This is the biblical doctrine of mature creation.

Chapter Nine

Superficial Appearance of Age

Growing Up Overnight.

Most everyone can remember the children's story of Jack and the Beanstalk. Young Jack was sent to the market to sell the family cow for some money, but instead was conned into buying some "magical" beans. Horrified and disgusted, his mother rebuked him for such a foolish act and threw the beans out of the kitchen window. The following morning when Jack looked out the window, there was a beanstalk which had grown high into the clouds above. The remainder of the story keeps children sitting on the edge of their seats. Of course, no one has ever seen anything grow up overnight, unless, of course, it happens in a Disney fantasy.

As much as man has sought to create a life in which every desire is fulfilled instantaneously through instant foods, remote controls and other technological marvels, he still recognizes that in this world growth and development are slow and deliberate. Growing up overnight only occurs in children's fairy tales and not in everyday life. However, is such an idea impossible with God?

"Light Trails."

By far the most common creationist answer to the dilemma about the age of the universe and the light coming from distant galaxies is that when God created the distant stars He created "light trails" connecting them to the Earth. In other words, when God created the stars and flung them into the heavens, the light waves may have been created fully extended, the light immediately spanning space to the Earth. Before you decide that such an idea is totally absurd, let me ask a simple question. What is more unbelievable and difficult to accomplish — creating light or moving light once it has been created? Or to put it another way, what is harder to do? Create and manufacture an automobile or move an automobile once it has been manufactured?

The Bible states that God is all powerful and that nothing is too difficult for Him. If God is the creator of light (He created the entire physical creation instantaneously and out of nothing), then surely He has the power and ability to instantly move that which He created.

When God created the universe, He made all things mature and fully functional. Scripture reveals that when God created man, he was fully grown, mature and had the appearance of age. And when God created the fruit trees, they offered ripe fruit immediately. God would not have created Adam, Eve and the animals and left them without food to eat while the grain, vegetables and fruit trees went through the growth, maturing and fruit-bearing processes we know today.

To the unbelieving skeptic, this probably is one of the most unacceptable explanations used by the creationist. To him this seems as ridiculous as the fable of Jack and the Beanstalk. Although there are other possibilities, no matter how reasonable any explanation may be, the atheistic evolutionist has already preset his mind against the possibility that God can exist. Therefore, all the evidence in the world will not make one speck of difference.

The creationists' reference to a "special creation with the superficial appearance of age" means that the physical laws which God used during creation week were very different laws than those we see operating in creation today. For this reason, there are limitations in the realm of nature today which did not exist during creation week. These limitations came into operation after the rebellion (fall) of man. It was at this time that the curse, or the law of decay known in physics as the second law of thermodynamics, took effect.

Once again the entire issue boils down to the question of God's existence. If God exists, then nothing is too difficult for Him. On the other hand, if He doesn't exist, then the unbelieving skeptic is free to be god and sit on the throne of his heart without fear of repercussion.

When is an Antique New?

Near the city of Dallas, Texas, where I was raised, there are many small country towns. Each usually has a general store selling new and used antiques. Such a combination of words seems contradictory. By definition, antiques cannot be new; and if they are new, then by definition, they cannot be antiques.

The term "new antiques" refers to items which appear to be very old but are actually brand new. For instance, there are specially designed tools which help make furniture look old. There is a drill for making holes that look like wormholes, and there is paint which makes things look antique.

I recently bought a dozen old-looking coins in Bethlehem. They appear to be coins from around the 1st century B.C. These coins look genuine; however, they are made for tourists. They appear to be very old and yet were made a very short time ago.

Two Ages.

There are numerous examples of newly produced products with two ages, the actual and the apparent. For example, there are the trendy fashions which attempt to create a well-worn look, although they are brand new. Presently designer jeans have such a look. Then there are homes and office buildings modeled after 18th-century architecture, and yet they have just been constructed. **(See fig. 17.)**

A "new antique" then, is an object created with both actual and apparent ages. Such was the case when God created Adam; he had two ages — the actual and the apparent. He *appeared* to be a mature adult. But his *actual* age would be calculated from the moment God breathed the breath of life into his nostrils (Gen. 2:7). We cannot even speak about creation from a biblical perspective without an understanding of the reality of a real age and a superficial age.

Figure 17. NEW ANTIQUES

The Purpose of Light.

All of God's creations had a superficial appearance of age as soon as they were created. When God created the stars, He created each with two ages — the actual age (new) and the apparent age (ancient). One of the reasons God created the stars was to give light to the Earth. So it is logical to assume the stars' light reached the Earth the moment they were created. The actual age of the light was "new"; however, the apparent age was "ancient."

Water into Wine.

Consider the miracle of Jesus' changing the water into wine. Mary, the mother of Jesus, approached her Son with a request for help. There was a need for more beverage for the wedding festivities. Jesus performed a miracle by turning plain water into wine. The miracle was of particular significance, which the guest of honor pointed out.

> ... and the master of the banquet tasted the water that had been turned into wine. He did not realize where it had come from, though the servants who had drawn the water knew. Then he called the bridegroom aside and said, "Everyone brings out the choice wine first and then the cheaper wine after the guests have had too much to drink; but you have saved the best till now" (John 2:9,10).

The custom at such occasions was to supply the most expensive and best wine at the beginning of the celebration, and when everyone had enjoyed their fill, then the less expensive and common selection of drink was provided. However, as the guest of honor of the feast noted, the quality of the wine served at the end of the wedding festivities was exceptional, meaning it was aged.

In the making of wine, after the fermentation process ceases within the grape, the juice goes through a maturing process for several months or years before it is considered of excellent quality. However, Jesus accomplished this transformation instantly. The wine, only minutes old, had the "taste" of age. It had an actual age (new) and an apparent age (old).

All Miracles of Christ Reveal a Superficial Appearance of Age.

All the miracles of Jesus illustrate the concept of the instantaneous having a "superficial appearance of age," and the revelation that God is capable of the impossible. Remember the man who was born blind and how Jesus restored his sight instantly? The skeptics who didn't believe in instantaneous healing had a problem accepting the story (John 9). Why? Because they were only accustomed to seeing the gradual process of the way things happen naturally.

During creation week, God commanded the Earth to bring forth fruit trees. He didn't create seeds first and then wait a number of years for them to grow to maturity. God's command resulted in the creation of fully mature objects that had a superficial appearance of age.

The whole cycle of life began with adult organisms rather than embryonic forms. To believe that the reverse is true requires an endless supply of miracles — a fertilized egg surviving outside of a mother's womb, infant mammals continuing to live without a mother's care and an endless number of other miracles far beyond that of Jack's beanstalk.

When the Earth was only one week old (actual age), there were mountains, valleys, sandy beaches and forests. Nature takes hundreds and thousands of years to form these phenomena (apparent age). But God created them instantaneously. Why is it so difficult for some to believe that God created the starlight to span instantly throughout the heavens and reach the Earth?

Chapter Ten

Taking a Bite Out of the Speed of Light

The Law of Decay.

There is an alternative solution to the idea of an instantaneous, mature creation. This alternative view doesn't invalidate the instantaneous "light trails." It has to do with the speed of light and the second law of thermodynamics — the physical law of decay called the "curse" in scripture.

One of the most strongly held evolutionary ideas is that the speed of light has been constant and unchanging throughout time. Such an assumption provides the evolutionist with the hope that radiometric dating will validate the theory of a universe 15-20 billion years old.

However, the Bible reveals that creation has been cursed (Genesis 3) and is therefore subject to the law of decay. As a result, things wear out, grow old and die, burn out and, in general, fall apart. All types of energy become useless after they are spent. **(See fig. 18.)** This includes every part of creation, including physical light (the electromagnetic spectrum) which was created on day one of the creation week. The stars were not created until day four. Not only is the energy which powers the stars' internal nuclear furnace being used up, but the light each star emits may have been gradually slowing down over the centuries.

The Speed of Light.

Is it possible then, that like every other part of creation, light is subject to the law of decay and has been slowing down? The evolutionary scientific establishment has assumed the constancy of the speed of light throughout time. But if light has been subject to the law of decay, then we have come upon one of the most staggering revelations known to science.

Throughout the history of scientific investigation there have been some one hundred published measurements of the speed of light. The first measurement was reported by the Danish astronomer Roemer in 1675. From that time to the present there have been numerous measurements of the speed of light.

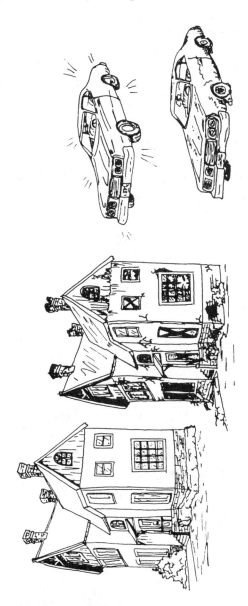

Figure 18. THE LAW OF DECAY

Barry Setterfield, an Australian astronomer and physicist, has done extensive research regarding the speed of light. His research seems to invalidate the assumption that the speed of light has been constant, and confirms the biblical truth that every part of creation is subject to the law of decay — including light.

Barry Setterfield examined the data regarding the speed of light, and much to his amazement, the results revealed a pattern of decay throughout the passage of time. So the speed of light has not been constant, as evolutionists thought. Setterfield's conclusions reveal that light traveled much faster in the past. Such a discovery should have been expected. Why would everything in creation be subject to the second law of thermodynamics (decay) except for one part — the electromagnetic spectrum, or light? There are no exceptions. The entire creation "groaneth" as God's Word declares (Rom. 8:22).

Although Setterfield was surprised at his findings, he soon learned that there had been others in the scientific community who had also noticed this decay trend. A number of scientists had seen the trend and concluded that light must have traveled much more rapidly in the past. Over the years there had been articles to this effect which had appeared in scientific literature. Nevertheless, the evolutionary establishment continued to assume the constancy of the speed of light in spite of the actual physical data that would suggest otherwise.[7] Such a startling revelation is, of course, controversial in the scientific community, even among creationists.

Staggering Revelation.

Setterfield created a graph based on the data from his research in order to determine light-speed measurements. This graph enabled him to estimate the speed of light backward to the point when the process of decay began shortly after the origin of the universe.

The graph indicates that the universe began about six thousand years ago — the same figure creationists have settled upon based on biblical chronologies and genealogies. The graph also indicates that at some point around 4,000 B.C., the speed of light approached an infinite velocity signifying the beginning of creation. Setterfield had expected the speed of light to be still showing a small decline today, but found that it became constant about 1960.

---

7 For the interested reader, Setterfield's layman's summaries on the topic may be obtained from Creation Science Foundation, P.O. Box 302, Sunnybank, QLD., 4109, Australia.

Post-Flood Decay Curve.

A similar decay curve and a final leveling off can be seen in man's life span after the Genesis Flood. Scripture reveals that up to the time of the Flood, the average life span of an individual was over 900 years. However, after the deluge and the simultaneous collapse of the pre-Flood canopy, man's life span dropped dramatically. It finally leveled out to "3 score and 10" years, which became the norm. **(See fig. 19.)**

Staggering Implications.

If Setterfield's calculations are correct, the implications are truly staggering. The furthest objects which astronomers can see from the Earth are called quasars. Quasars are stars which, when calculated by the current speed of light, are considered to be 10 billion light years away. However, using Setterfield's findings on the velocity of light, because light was traveling much faster at the beginning of creation, the light could have reached Earth in 6,000 years. This is further evidence that our universe is only about 6,000 years old. By Setterfield's calculations, on creation day, the speed of light was so great that light traveled the 50,000 light-years from the

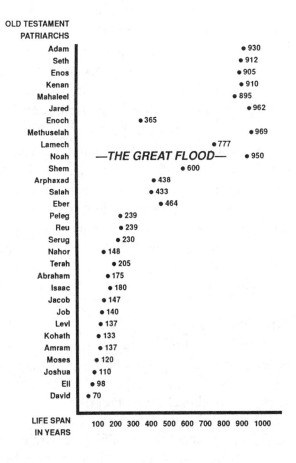

Figure 19. POST-FLOOD DECAY CURVE

center of our galaxy to the Earth in just 3.2 seconds. **(See fig. 20.)** In other words, the speed of light was infinite or instantaneous. Such a disclosure devastates evolutionism and its assumption of an ancient universe.

At this point, no doubt this question has crossed your mind: What about radiometric dating? Hasn't carbon-14 and radioactive uranium dating proven that the Earth is billions of years old? We shall investigate this "sacred cow" of evolutionism in Volume IX, covering in full radioactive dating and the assumptions and flaws associated with each method used in dating rocks, bones and fossils. In the remaining pages of this volume, we shall look at a number of additional clocks which testify to a young Earth and young creation.

The Final Word....

Barry Setterfield's work forces one to consider interesting possibilities: Is there a Creator? Is the universe young, which would substantiate biblical chronology?

Setterfield's work is exciting. But of course, no theory is without the possibility of flaw, even if it beautifully matches the truth of scripture. So, although it is difficult to see how, future

Figure 20. LIGHTWARP SPEED

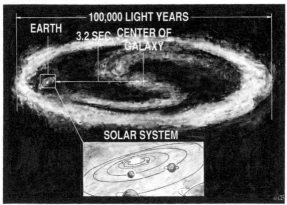

discovery may show it to be incorrect. Even if this should happen, the lesson it shows will have been extremely valuable. Just as the mighty walls of Jericho came suddenly tumbling down, a simple discovery in science is capable of demolishing an entire sacred edifice of supposedly unshakable certainty. It seems the story of Jack and his beanstalk is closer to the truth than the 21st-century myth of evolutionism.

PART III
YOUNG EARTH CLOCKS

Chapter Eleven

Testimonies of Young Earth Clocks

Figure 21. YOUNG EARTH CLOCKS

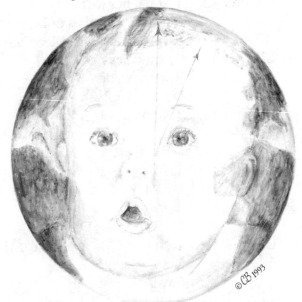

Scientists are learning that many of the theories about Earth's origins must be revised.

Dr. Murray, former director of the Jet Propulsion Laboratory in Pasadena, California and the architect of many of the United States' planetary missions, acknowledged that the whole concept of the early history of the Earth is being reevaluated.

The evidence in support of a young universe has grown rapidly in recent years as a result of the explosion of data gleaned from the tremendous advances in technology. For evolutionists, the outcome of the U.S. space exploration has been a bombshell producing a series of shocks and revelations. Phrases such as "apparent paradox" and "seems to violate known laws of physics" have filled the articles written by evolutionists. Of course the discoveries fully agree with the Word of God and the basic laws of physics as long as one is willing to give up the idea of immense ages. The findings are clear and simple. Creation is not old; it is young.

In spite of so much evidence to the contrary, the prevailing evolutionary dogma continues to deceive those in the scientific community as well as students who fall prey to those who teach it as truth. The primary reason for this headlock is that the only alternative is to acknowledge God, which is unthinkable for the atheistic heart.

Besides the whale found on its tail and the missing dust on the moon, many additional evidences testify to a young creation. At least 80 different natural clocks (ways to date the Earth and the universe) testify to a recent creation. However, these are ignored or explained away by evolutionists. Thirty of these clocks of nature are covered in this volume. Genesis chapter one asserts that God created everything with the "appearance of age." This idea definitely throws a kink into the evolutionists' works. Because they refuse to believe in God or in His Word, some clocks used by evolutionists are not accurate. More will be said about this in Volume IX of the Creation Science Series entitled, *The Dismantling of Evolutionism's Sacred Cow: Radiometric Dating.*

Chapter Twelve

Testimony Five: The Shrinking Sun

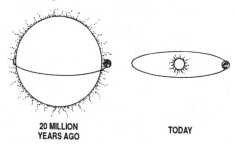

Figure 22. THE SHRINKING SUN

20 MILLION YEARS AGO   **TODAY**

Not in a Million Years.

Did you know the sun is shrinking in size? This creates another problem for the evolutionist. Projecting backwards in time just one million years, which is far less than the estimated age proposed by evolutionists, we discover that the great size the sun would have been if it had existed then and the amount of deadly radiation it would have transmitted would have made life on Earth impossible.

An *Associated Press* news wire report of
March 23, 1980 made this surprising statement:

> The sun's diameter appears to have
> been decreasing by about one tenth
> percent per century.

Major newspapers across the country
bannered this headline: "The sun is shrinking."
This news story by Kevin McKean reported the
results of research studies by solar specialist Jack
Eddy of the Harvard-Smithsonian Center for
Astrophysics and the National Center for
Atmospheric Research and mathematician Aram
Boornazian. Through examination of records
kept by the British Royal Observatory since
1750, Eddy and Boornazian concluded that the
sun appears to be shrinking at a rate of about
one-tenth of a percent per century.[8] Scientists
have been observing the sun for over one
hundred years; the evidence seems conclusive.
Every hour that passes, our sun shrinks about
five feet.

Of course five feet an hour isn't much when
you consider the sun is 840,000 miles in
diameter. But what are the implications? If you
believe the Earth's age is only 6,000 years,
there's no problem. In that span of time the sun

---

8   *Physics Today*, No. 9, Sept. 1979.

would have shrunk only 6%. But how can you contend with the shrinkage if you believe the billions of years idea? If the sun existed only 100,000 years ago it would have been double its present diameter. And only twenty million years ago (not to mention 4½ billion years that evolutionists claim for the age of the Earth) the surface of the sun would have been *touching the Earth*. **(See fig. 23.)**

As far as researchers can tell, this rate of shrinkage has been consistent since the origin of the sun. But astronomers acknowledge that there are stars much larger than the present size of our sun which burn much hotter and faster than the sun. This means that the sun may have shrunk much more than is realized, creating an even greater problem for the evolutionary myth of a 4½-billion-year-old solar system. There was only one Son 4½ billion years ago: the Son of God! From this simple evidence it is clear that life on Earth one million years ago would have been totally impossible.

Figure 23. A CLOSER LOOK

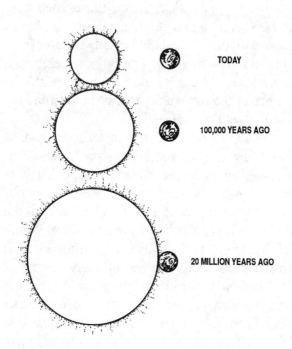

TODAY

100,000 YEARS AGO

20 MILLION YEARS AGO

Chapter Thirteen

Testimonies 6-7: The Mid-Life Maladies of Mother Earth and Ol' Man Moon

Figure 24. "DUNLAPS' DISEASE"

©CB 1993

"Dunlaps' Disease" and Other Mid-Life Maladies.

Some physical features of a person indicate his age. "Dunlaps' disease" is a sign of middle age —"when the belly done laps over the belt." This is also known as the battle of the bulge. Another age indicator occurs when one is robbed of his locks and ends up with a receding hairline. Both features are obvious indicators of age. They are signs of maturity.

Likewise, two similar indicators in the physical world act as natural clocks which help us to determine the age of the Earth: the bulge around the Earth's midsection and the receding moon. These features provide us with clues regarding the age of the Earth.

Figure 25. THE MIDDLE-AGED EARTH

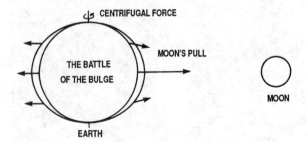

Testimony 6: The Battle of the Bulge.

Atomic clocks show that the rate of the Earth's spin has been decreasing. These precision clocks have been used for many years to measure the Earth's spin rate to the nearest billionth of a second. They have consistently found that the Earth is slowing down at the rate of one second per year. If the Earth is billions of years old, the rate at which it was initially spinning would have been so great that centrifugal force would have seriously deformed the Earth. Even 500,000 years ago the Earth would have been spinning so fast that the equator would have developed a bulge much greater than the one it has.

If the Earth is as old as evolutionists claim, where's the bulge? "Dunlaps' disease" has not yet occurred on planet Earth, so the Earth is not middle-aged, old or ancient. It has to be younger than 500,000 years — a long way from the 4½ billion years evolutionists insist upon. A 500,000-year-old Earth compared to a 4½-billion-year-old Earth is the equivalent of a 1-year-old child compared to an 18,000-year-old man. Thus, it's quite obvious why "Dunlaps' disease" has not set in on the Earth's midsection. All that can be seen is a little bit of baby fat, or only what accounts for a few thousand years.

Figure 26. THE FINAL ECLIPSE OF THE MOON

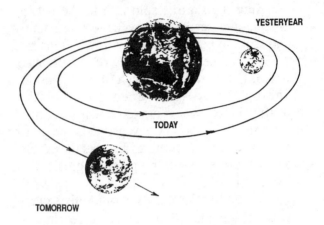

Testimony 7: The Receding Locks.

Another indicator of middle age is a thinning or receding hairline. This receding indicator also occurs with Earth's moon. Scientists observe that such things as tidal friction from the ocean's changing tides each day are causing the Earth's rotational speed to slow down a very tiny amount each year. This minute slowdown causes the moon's distance from the earth to increase by just under two inches per year as it spirals outward away from the Earth. **(See fig. 27.)** In other words, the old man in the moon is receding with age much like the hair on a middle-aged male. Two inches a year may not sound like much, but calculating back, the moon would have been touching Earth only 1.4 billion years ago. That is ridiculous, even from an evolutionary standpoint. And if the Earth were 4.5 billion years old, starting with a realistic separation between the Earth and the moon, at the present rate of separation, the moon would be completely out of sight by now. **(See fig. 28.)**

From a creationistic perspective, the moon was probably put in place close to its present distance from the Earth. If the age of the pair is a maximum of 10,000 years, then the distance of the moon's recession from the Earth would be less than a mile.

The moon presents numerous other problems for the theory of evolutionism. For instance, where did it come from? Earth's moon is much larger than a satellite usually is in comparison to its mother planet. The Earth could not have captured the moon while it was flying through space; its orbit is too perfectly round. It couldn't have broken off from the Earth at some "early stage"; its mineral composition is too different from the Earth's. The moon is one-third less dense than the Earth, so it couldn't have been

Figure 27. 2 INCHES A YEAR

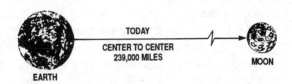

formed from the same material as the Earth. No acceptable evolutionary explanation can be found for the origin of the moon. However, there is one from a biblical standpoint:

> God made two great lights—the greater light to govern the day and the lesser light to govern the night. He also made the stars (Gen. 1:16).

Figure 28. KISSING BY THE LIGHT OF THE MOON

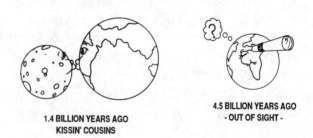

Chapter Fourteen

Testimonies 8-9: Romantic and Magnetic Decay

Figure 29. A HEAVENLY ATTRACTION

©CB 1993

Testimony 8: The Decaying Magnetic Earth.

The word magnetism brings to mind rhapsodies of romance and irresistible attraction.

God created a strong desire between the sexes. This attraction was designed to culminate in marriage. But no matter how captivating one's beauty, in time gravity takes over and results in sags, bags, bifocals, bulges, bunyons, brown spots and baldness. Only the power of the Holy Spirit can strengthen one's attraction in a marriage relationship when beauty fades with age.

Likewise, there is a powerful magnetism surrounding the Earth which is fading with age. This magnetic field enables man to navigate with the help of a magnetic compass, which always points to the magnetic North Pole. The source of this field is the electric currents which run from pole to pole in the Earth's core.

The Earth's magnetic field is a clock; it can tell us something about the Earth's age. As with everything else in the universe, the second law of thermodynamics, better known as the law of decay, is in operation in the magnetic field.

Physicist Dr. Thomas Barnes, Professor of Physics at the University of Texas and a consultant to Globe Universal Scientists Inc., points out that the Earth's magnetic field has been decaying since it was first measured in

1835. Dr. Barnes reveals that the magnetic field has an estimated half-life of 1,400 years. In other words, every 1,400 years it loses half of its strength. According to observation and predictions, the magnetic field will virtually vanish as early as 3,180 A.D.[9] The magnetic field's strength is weakening as a result of resistance from friction and heat loss.

What is more important to our study is Dr. Barnes' findings regarding the strength of the field in the past:

1. 1,400 years ago it would have been twice as strong as now.
2. In 825 B.C., or 2,800 years ago, it would have been four times greater than it is today.
3. In 2,225 B.C. it would have been 8 times greater.
4. 10,000 years ago the magnetic field would have been so strong that life could not have existed.
5. 20,000 years ago the field would have been 8,000 times as strong as it is today, so strong that the mantle and core of the Earth could not have held together.
6. One million years ago the Earth would have been a vapor as a result of the enormous heat generated from the magnetic field. (See fig. 30.)

9   *Science News,* June 28, 1980.

Figure 30. MAGNETIC MEASUREMENTS

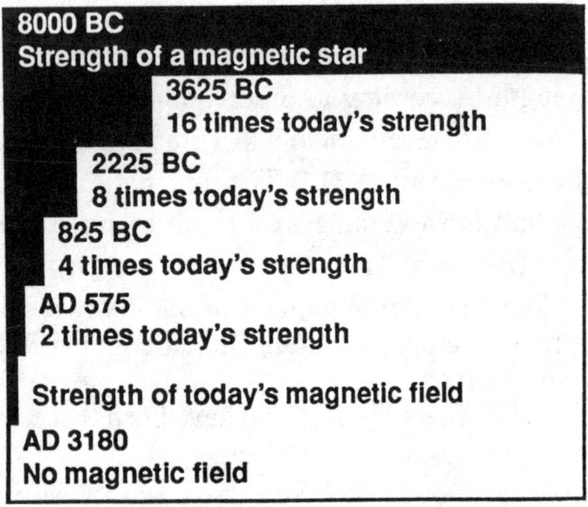

8000 BC
Strength of a magnetic star

3625 BC
16 times today's strength

2225 BC
8 times today's strength

825 BC
4 times today's strength

AD 575
2 times today's strength

Strength of today's magnetic field

AD 3180
No magnetic field

If the half-life of the magnetic field is truly what Dr. Barnes has calculated from his careful measurements, the Earth's magnetic field would have been equal to that of a magnetic star as little as 10,000 years ago. The magnetic power generated by a magnetic star is so great that life would be an impossibility. According to Dr. Barnes, to be consistent with the laws of physics, and assuming the magnetic field has continually weakened, we can only conclude that life on Earth would not have been possible 10,000 years ago. The decay rate of the magnetic field reveals the Earth to be very young.

Testimony 9: The Core of the Earth.

Associated with the decaying magnetic field is the heat within the Earth's core. **(See fig. 31.)** This heat is escaping through the planet's surface. Calculating what the temperature would have been 10,000 years ago, life could not have existed on Earth as the heat would have been too extreme.

The Earth under a strong magnetic field would be like an animal struck by a powerful lightning bolt. A strong magnetic field has something in common with electricity: both have the potential to destroy life as a result of the extreme heat they generate.

The heat produced by the currents associated with a magnetic field of the strength discussed earlier would have been 250 million times the heat found in the Earth's core today. Dr. Barnes points out, "It is not very plausible that the core of the Earth could have stayed together under those conditions. It would appear from these arguments that the origin of the Earth's magnetic moment is much less than 20,000 years ago."[10]

---

10 *Science News*, June 28, 1980.

Figure 31. A FIERY FURNACE

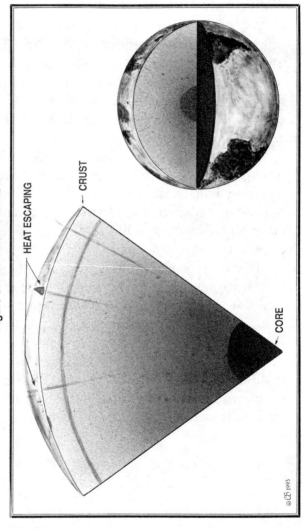

HEAT ESCAPING

CRUST

CORE

Chapter Fifteen

Testimonies 10-14: Salt, Silt, Sediment and a Scourging Surge

Figure 32. SODIUM CHLORIDE

SALT

Testimony 10: Oceans.

Back in the 1800s when evolutionists first began to look for ways to validate their belief in immense eons for the age of the Earth, they thought that the content of sodium chloride (common table salt) in the oceans would indicate the Earth's age. So they measured the annual rate of salt flow into the oceans from all the world's rivers. Then they calculated the amount of salt in the oceans and divided the annual flow into that amount. They assumed that the oceans had no salt in the beginning and that the rivers always carried salt at their present rate. However, such assumptions cannot be verified.

The results of their study led to a quick drop of the subject. Why were the conclusions discarded by the evolutionists? Because no one likes salt rubbed into their wounds. The conclusions of the study were detrimental to the theory of evolutionism. The investigation yielded a *maximum* of 100 million years for the age of the oceans. This is a far cry from what the evolutionists were hoping to find; they were looking for a clock that would read billions of years to support their theory.

Actually, new data reveals that the amount of salt in the oceans — as well as in the Dead Sea in Israel — is under thirteen thousand years. Measuring uranium salts instead of sodium chloride indicates only 10,000 years.

Testimony 11: Barrier Reef Silt.

Corals are tiny colonies of marine organisms which live together in warm and shallow water. Every diver knows that the variety, color and shape of coral formations is spectacular to behold. Each coral is formed from limestone by the tiny organisms into a kind of skeleton. Each generation builds on the last, eventually forming rocky ridges called a coral reef. The growth rate in coral has been generally assumed to be very slow. Near Key West, Florida, reefs are presently growing about a half-inch per year. Large reefs, therefore, are presumed to be very old. However, there is new evidence that coral structures may grow at a much faster rate if conditions are favorable. For example, in the 1970s it was discovered that a coral on a bow gun of a ship which was sunk in 1944 during World War II is five feet in diameter. (*National Geographic*, May 1976, pp. 578-613).

Scientists involved in a worldwide $65-million-a-year effort to plumb the secrets of the ocean say Australia's Great Barrier Reef is possibly younger than 500,000 years. Until recently they believed it was 20 million years old — that's 40 times the actual age.

Scientists now say the reef is too new to yield commercial quantities of oil or gas. Expedition

Figure 33. GREAT BARRIER REEF

co-leader Dr. Peter Davies said test drilling off the seaward face of the reef had also shown that the underlying sediment essential to hydrocarbon (petroleum) development was significantly younger than expected.[11]

In addition, research has been done on the reef by taking core samples and counting the hundreds of layers that have been built one on top of the other. Rivers along the coast of the region of Queensland flood annually because of their tropical location. Each flood deposits a fine layer of silt on the reef. By boring through to the bottom of the reef, scientists have been able to ascertain its age by simply counting the layers — a method similar to counting the rings on a tree. The age of the reef has been determined to be only a few thousand years old. Such an age lines up well with the biblical position of a recent creation.

Figure 34. A GREAT BURIAL REEF

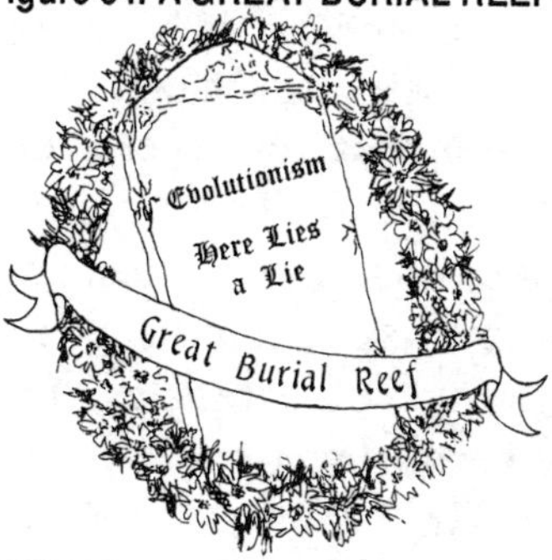

Evolutionism
Here Lies
a Lie

Great Burial Reef

---

11 *The Sun* (Brisbane, Australia), Oct. 15, 1990 (p. 3)

Testimony 12: River Sediment.

Another clock pertains to the rivers of the world. One can usually date a river by its delta — the accumulation of sediment that builds up at the end of a river where it empties into a lake or an ocean. One can date the age of America's longest and largest river, the Mississippi, by dating its delta — the place where it flows into the Gulf of Mexico. The age of the river can be calculated by dividing the total volume of sediment already present in the delta by the amount of sediment entering per year.

These calculations are correct only if the rate of the sediment entering the delta has remained constant throughout time. On the other hand, if at some time in the past there was a massive worldwide flood catastrophe, a lot more sediment would have been swept into the delta in a very short period of time. Calculations made as previously mentioned would be wrong; the river would appear much older than it is.

The Mississippi River has been observed for hundreds of years, and all sorts of measurements have been taken on its flow. Depending on which evolutionist one asks about its age, there is an extensive range of estimates. In 1853 Sir Charles Lyell estimated the river's age at around 60,000 years. In 1967 Wyckoff, in his book

Figure 35. THE MISSISSIPPI DELTA

MISSISSIPPI DELTA

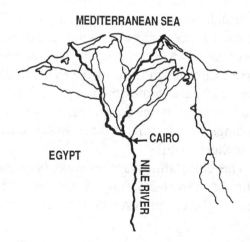

MEDITERRANEAN SEA

CAIRO

EGYPT

NILE RIVER

Principles of Geology put it at about 25 million years.

According to the U.S. Army Corps of Engineers, the average depth is only 40 feet and the surface area of the delta is 30,000 square miles. The calculated rate of addition of sediment is roughly 7.3 billion cubic feet per year. Dividing the volume of silt by the rate of silt flow shows the age of the Mississippi River to be 4,563 years. This is a far cry from 25 million years. This "young age" is very embarrassing to an evolutionist. Several additional ways may be used to check out the age of a river; these other methods confirm that the above calculations are valid.

The Mississippi is not the only river for which calculations indicate a young age. It is also true for the deltas of the Danube, Nile, Rhone, Rhine and other major rivers of the world. They all reveal a very young age. Before the construction of the Aswan Dam in Egypt, a measurement of the sediment deposited by the Nile's flooding each year gave a maximum age of less than 30,000 years. Just one or two larger-than-normal floodings would bring the calculations close to the biblical record.

The calculations above have been made using the present-day flow of the rivers. However, if there were tremendous catastrophic changes in the past, the rate of sedimentation would have accelerated, and these calculations would be off. Adjusting the average flow of sediment to take this into account, it appears the rivers of the world are quite young. In fact, the calculations reveal the Earth's rivers came into being about the time of Noah's Flood.

Testimony 13: Ocean Sediment.

Evolutionism teaches that when life first appeared, the Earth was probably covered entirely by water. In time, land somehow appeared. The rain caused the formation of the rivers, which returned the water into the sea. Somehow in all of this, the formation of the sediments on the ocean floors came into being.

Scientists tell us that every year 28 billion tons of sediment are being washed off the land into the oceans. The formation of sediments at their present rate of accumulation requires only 33 million years, not the 4½ billion which evolutionists assign as the Earth's age. If the ocean were only one billion years old, there would be an 18-mile-deep layer of sediment on the ocean floor. In fact, the layer of sediment would be 100 miles thick if the Earth were as old as evolutionists claim. But, there is only about a half mile of sediment covering the volcanic rock on the sea beds. **(See fig. 36.)** And from a creationist's

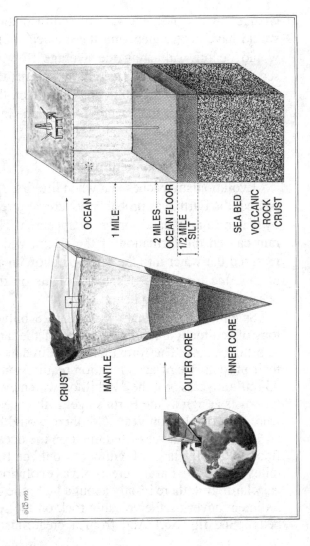

Figure 36. MISSING SEDIMENT

CRUST

MANTLE

OUTER CORE

INNER CORE

OCEAN

1 MILE

2 MILES
OCEAN FLOOR

1/2 MILE
SILT

SEA BED

VOLCANIC
ROCK
CRUST

viewpoint the major part of the oceans' sediments were laid down during the year of the Flood catastrophe.

Of the elements found in the oceans, at the present rate of accumulation, 29 require 10,000 years or less to accumulate and 8 require 100,000 years or less. It looks as if the Earth is much younger than evolutionists have claimed.

Testimony 14: Niagara Surge.

Figure 37. NIAGARA FALLS

The famous waterfall, Niagara Falls, is a magnificent example of a geo-clock that reveals a very young Earth. The rim of the Falls is eroding at a known rate every year. **(See fig. 38.)** The Falls lie on one of the connecting rivers

Figure 38. YEARLY EROSION OF FALLS

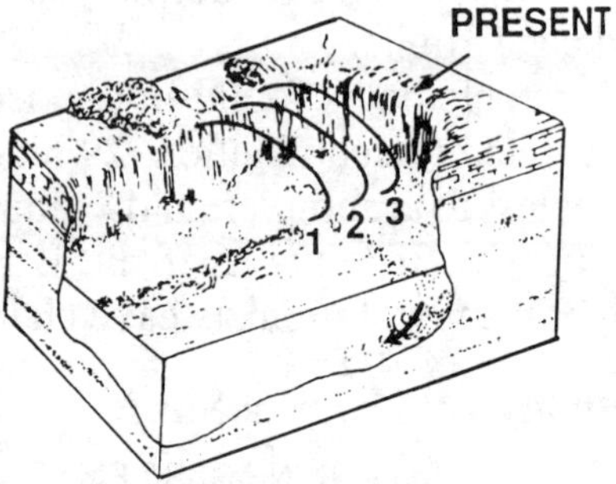

1. 1700
2. 1800
3. 1900

between two of the Great Lakes of North America — Lake Erie and Lake Ontario.

The Falls have eroded their way 10 miles upstream since they were first formed. **(See fig. 39.)** The enormous volume of surging water eats through the limestone base relatively rapidly; and if erosion continues at its present rate, geologists estimate that the Falls will disappear completely in about 22,000 years.

Each year the water erodes the base about 6 feet. Calculations reveal these Falls were formed no earlier than 10,000 years ago. This is true, of course, only if the water has been flowing over Niagara Falls at a consistent rate — the speed at which it presently flows. Creationists believe the water flowed much faster shortly after the Flood of Noah. Creation geologists believe it has only

Figure 39. TOTAL EROSION OF FALLS

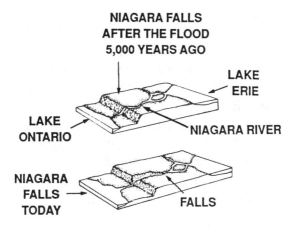

taken about 5,000 years to erode from its original precipice.

Conclusion.

Here we have a series of testimonies, all of which conclude that the Earth is of a recent origin. These evidences bury evolutionism with salt, silt, sediment and a scourging surge. You would think that with such a covering it would have long since become fossilized. However, evolutionism will continue in its attempt to dig itself out of each pit by belittling any geo-clocks which do not harmonize with their geological charts. Any such clock will be ignored or explained away. Evolutionists had decided that the Earth is billions of years old before they ever began searching for clues to the Earth's age. Their theory requires billions of years to have any possibility of being accepted as credible. Of course, the heart of the issue is not time, but rather the Father of Time, God. No matter how many evidences there are in favor of a young Earth, there will never be enough to convince the mind of an individual who doesn't want anyone to sit on the throne of his kingdom except himself. The real issue is one of the heart.

Chapter Sixteen

Testimonies 15-18: Soil and Oil

Testimony 15: Continent and Mountain Erosion.

Another indicator of a young Earth involves the present rate at which the world's land masses are slowly eroding into the oceans. **(See fig. 40.)** Continental geography indicates that past rates of erosion were much greater than today's. If the oceans have been in existence for just one billion years, at the present rate of erosion at least 30 times more sediment should have accumulated in them. All the Earth's mountain ranges should have eroded into the sea in about 14 million years, which is less than $\frac{1}{2}$ of 1% of the $4\frac{1}{2}$ billion years of Earth's history according to evolutionists. Thus, once again we have another discrepancy in the evolutionary assumption that the Earth is billions of years old.

Figure 40. MOUNTAIN REMOVAL

Figure 40. MOUNTAIN REMOVAL (cont.)

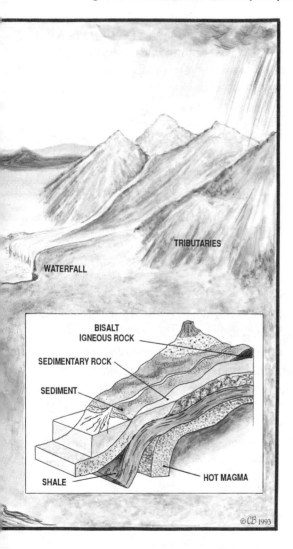

Testimony 16: Soil Production.

The soil which sustains plant life on Earth lies over the face of the land in a thin layer an average of seven or eight inches deep. The Earth beneath that top layer is as dead and sterile as the moon. A thin layer of top soil is all that stands between man and extinction. So how long does it take for top soil to accumulate?

Scientists estimate that the combination of plant growth, bacterial decay and erosion produces six inches of top soil in 5,000-20,000 years. If the physical processes of the Earth have continued the same as they are today for millions of years, why isn't more top soil found? Once again we see a testimony in favor of a young Earth.

Testimony 17: Petroleum Pressure.

What happens when drillers hit a pocket of crude oil deep within the Earth? The black liquid comes gushing up. Occasionally there is a mechanical failure in the equipment and the unharnessed petroleum spews out hundreds of feet into the air. Such a blast is a result of the tremendous pressure trapped below in the sedimentary rocks. As time passes, the pressure begins to dissipate as the surrounding rocks begin to absorb the oil like a sponge absorbs water.

Figure 41. DISSIPATING DEPOSITS OF BLACK GOLD

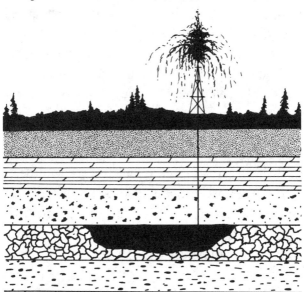

Rocks differ in porosity (the absorption rate). However, even the densest rocks have some degree of porosity, and in time will begin absorbing the oil, causing the oil pocket to lose its tremendous pressure. Scientists are aware that these forceful pressure pockets are gradually diminishing, much like air which slowly seeps from the tire of an automobile.

Today, some high-pressured wells have an incredible 16,000 pounds per square inch of pressure at the surface. For example, when the

700 Kuwaiti oil wells were sabotaged by Iraq during the 1991 Gulf War, the explosions caused oil to spurt out of the ground at 600-800 mph, burning up to 30,000 barrels of oil per day. This would have continued at the same rate for the next 50 years, if the wells had been left uncapped.

A pocket of oil 2-3 miles below ground has far greater pressure per square inch. So how long will it take for the most intense pressure deep within the Earth to completely dissipate? Experts in the oil industry tell us that a maximum of 10,000 years is needed before the most intense pressure completely dissipates into the most dense rock.

Dr. Melvin Cook, who served as a professor at the University of Utah and President of IRECO Chemicals (1968 winner of the Nitro Nobel Award), reported: "... the permeability of the rock above the trapped high pressure fluid zone ... is so high even in the tightest traps that the fluid will leak out of the formation at the prevailing pressures in only a few thousand years." (*Bible-Science Newsletter*, Jan. 15, 1970). This statement by such a notable professional is compelling evidence for a young Earth.

If the Earth were more than 10,000 years old, even the highest amount of pressure would have been completely absorbed into the surrounding rock. Evolutionism has dated the formation of oil reserves at several hundred million years. If that were accurate, the oil pressure should have dissipated long ago; yet we still find extreme pressure from oil wells. Here we have another testimony for a young Earth.

Figure 42. EXTRATERRESTRIAL MATTER

Testimony 18: Meteorite Material.

Scientists continually announce newly-detected asteroids in our solar system. Thousands have been detected, and there is growing concern that in the not-too-distant future one of the large ones will collide with the Earth. Now it is

believed by the evolutionary scientific community that throughout the Earth's supposed
4½-billion-year history large meteorites have
impacted from time to time — such as the one
that left a ½-mile-wide crater in Arizona. **(See
fig. 43.)**

Although evolutionists say 50,000 years may
have passed between each major impact, in 4½
billion years there would have been tens of thousands of major impacts and hundreds of
thousands of minor ones such as we see on the
cratered surface of the moon. There is only one
minor problem with this evolutionary notion —
there just is no evidence to substantiate such a
myth.

In "older" geologic formations, no signs
whatsoever of the presence of meteorites have
been found. Billions and billions of tons of coal
and other minerals have been mined all around
the world, and only rare incidences of meteoritic
material have been reported by professionals in
the mining industry. By and large, meteorites
have not been found in the geologic column
except in the top layer of strata. **(See fig. 44.)**

How is it that until recently the Earth has
escaped meteorites plunging to its surface?
Large numbers of meteorites should be
embedded in the thousands of feet of
sedimentary rock which blanket much of the

Figure 43. METEOR CRATER, ARIZONA

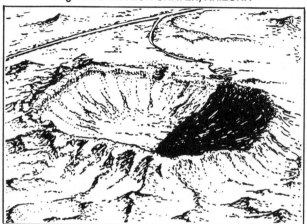

Earth and which, according to the evolutionary time chart, took several billion years for their deposition.

The absence of meteorites in the sedimentary rock fits well with Flood geology. Creationists believe the major sedimentary strata were deposited during the time of Noah's Flood. During the year of the Flood, only a small number of meteorites fell and were entrapped in the Flood sediments. Many more meteorites have fallen in the thousands of years since the Flood, and some of these should have been preserved from erosion. As a matter of fact that is just the case. Many have been found and are on display in museums around the world. Here again we find evidence for a young Earth.

Figure 44. MISSING METEORITES

Chapter Seventeen

Testimony 19:
God's Enormous Flagpoles

Living Giants.

By far the tallest living things found on Earth are redwood trees. Some stand taller than a 35-story building. Like all trees, redwoods continue to grow as long as they are alive. Thus, the longer a tree lives, the taller and wider it becomes.

The most famous redwood tree in the world is called General Sherman. Located in Sequoia National Park in California, it is almost as tall as a 30-story building. It has been around for nearly 4,000 years. To support its height, its immense trunk is so large that 17 men stretching out their arms could just about reach around it. This single tree contains enough wood to construct 100 homes.

Except for earthquakes, strong winds, and men who cut them down for timber, redwoods

Figure 45. GOD'S OWN FLAGPOLES

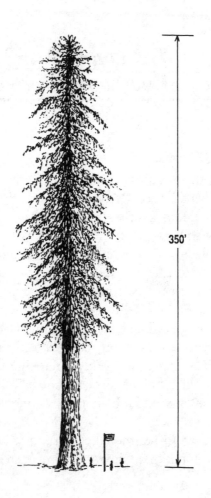

350'

and sequoias have few enemies. Scientists have researched the redwoods carefully, and have not found even one that has died of old age, sickness, or insect attack. Insects are normally a common problem for trees. For instance, the Dutch elm disease killed thousands of beautiful shade trees in many American small towns. In the past, in certain areas of Florida and some islands in the Caribbean, palm trees have been totally wiped out by disease.

Since redwoods seem to be so impervious to attack, it is significant that no redwood tree has been found older than about 4,000 years. There are, though, many redwoods in the 3,000-year-old range.

Bristlecone Pine Trees.

But as tall and old as many redwoods are, it is not a redwood that is the oldest tree known. A bristlecone pine in the white mountains of California has this honor. It is more than 4,000 years old.

In the White Mountains east of the Sierra Nevada range near Bishop, California, there are trees still standing that were growing for centuries before Moses received the Ten Commandments. Their annual growth rings give a reasonably accurate idea of their ages. These twisted and weather-beaten bristlecone pine trees cling stubbornly to life in one of the most hostile environments on Earth. High in the arid desert of Nevada, these rare and rugged trees have been growing for about 5,000 years. Because of the hardiness of the bristlecone trees, they could likely go on living for thousands of years to come, barring catastrophe.

The oldest tree in the Schulman grove, named the Methuselah tree, has 4,700 rings. That means it was a sprouting seedling about the time Noah climbed out of the Ark. **(See fig. 46.)**

If the bristlecone pines and the redwoods do not die of old age, why aren't there living specimens much older than approximately 4,500 years? Why aren't there groves of trees 5,000 or 7,000 or even 10,000 years old? If these hearty trees have lived 5,000 years, they could certainly have lived longer. It is evident that they have lived in the past because they have been found fossilized in layers of rock, which according to evolutionism are millions of years old. It's almost as though all these trees living today were planted on a virgin Earth just 5,000 years ago. Apparently, the trees that grew before 5,000 years ago were wiped out by a catastrophic natural disaster.

Figure 46. RECORD OF THE REDWOODS

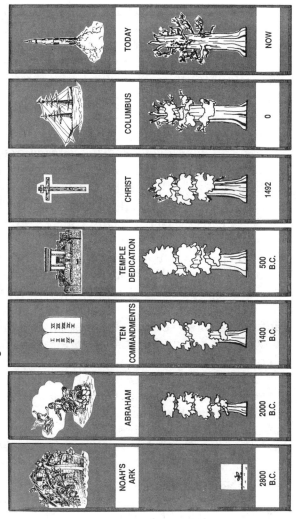

This is strong evidence for Noah's Flood having occurred around 5,000 years ago. The Bible gives a clear historical record pointing to a global Flood. It stands to reason that the trees of greatest longevity would date back only to that time and no further.

Spiritual Parallel.

The giant redwoods make an additional statement. Their thick bark protects them against fire, insects, plague. Christians likewise should have a thick bark (shield of faith) to protect them against the enemy's attacks. Young redwoods have the ability to grow in semi-lighted areas, which makes it possible for them to become the strongest, tallest trees. Believers who have gone through the darkness victoriously can be pillars of strength — great encouragers and counselors — because they not only have the power of the Holy Spirit, but empathy and understanding.

Redwoods must grow in groups because they have shallow root systems which are only five to ten feet deep. They must grow in groves with their roots linked together so they can protect one another from the wind. Isolated, they do not have the networking of roots to protect them. Likewise, isolated young or weak Christians become easy targets for the enemy. The winds of adversity can destroy them.

When a bristlecone pine for some reason or another succumbs to the elements and finally dies after three or four thousand years, it does not decay and fall to the ground like most trees. It continues to stand for another thousand years or so. The elements merely wear away the bark and polish the wood until it glistens like a white statue, still testifying to the strength that comes from enduring adversity. Like the bristlecone pine, if we are faithful through the trials, our lives will continue to testify long after we have left this Earth. We will be like Abel, the righteous man whose offerings were commended by the Lord: "By faith he still speaks, even though he is dead" (Heb. 11:4).

Chapter Eighteen

Testimony 20: "Apeman" Art and Catacomb Cavern Formations

Something's Wrong Somewhere.

Have you ever read about cave paintings dated at tens of thousands of years old and wondered how Mr. Neanderthal manufactured paint that could last all that time on a soggy cave wall? After one such story appeared in *The Australian* newspaper, a reader wrote a letter to the editor:

> Twenty years ago I painted my house with the best materials available to me. After 20 years the interior of the laundry room is in sad need of paint renewal, but I was satisfied with this seeming longevity. Now I read that a Tasmanian aboriginal took some

powdered red ochre and blew it
through a hollow bone onto a soggy
cave wall and it has lasted for 20,000
years. Something's wrong somewhere. Where can I get a can of that
stuff?

It is amazing what a little common sense can
do. It enables one to see through the fantasies of
highly educated men who "profess to be wise
and yet become fools" (Rom. 1:22).

Cave Formations.

Figure 48. 'TITES AND 'MITES

©CB 1993

How long does it take for a stalactite to grow?
Evolutionists have claimed that eons of time are
required for one cubic inch of a stalactite to form.

It is generally assumed that it takes about 100 years for the formation of one inch of a stalactite or a stalagmite. Accordingly, it is argued, millions of years must have been required for huge formations to develop. Carlsbad Caverns are said to have begun forming about 60 million years ago — according to the evolutionary geology. Stalactites are formed by the evaporation of lime-bearing waters which percolate through the cavern roof. Obviously, the rate of formation of stalactites depends mainly on:
1. Rate of water drip.
2. The amount of minerals in the water.
3. The rate of evaporation of water.

In some caves, the rate of evaporation is very slow. This is the case at Carlsbad Caverns National Park in New Mexico — located in an arid part of the world. But the rate has not necessarily always been so slow. The rate of water drip probably was much greater immediately after the Flood when the ground was completely saturated. With the gradual reduction of the water table, it is obvious that the percolating waters were for some time quite plentiful, gradually lessening over time. Thus the rate of formation of stalactites and stalagmites would have been rapid at first, gradually leveling off to the present rate.

Frozen in Time.

Interestingly, there is more than a little evidence that cave formations can grow rapidly, even today, if conditions are right. In October 1953, *National Geographic* published a photo of a bat that had fallen and been cemented on a stalagmite in the famous Carlsbad Caverns. The stalagmite had grown so fast it was able to preserve the bat before the creature had time to decompose. **(See fig. 49.)**

The fact that a bat could be cemented inside a stalagmite supplies an important clue to stalagmite growth rate. Evidently, formation sometimes occurs quite rapidly. So actually, the growth of dripstone formations can, under certain conditions, be described as catastrophic.

Stalactites are found even in man-made tunnels only a few years old. A photograph taken in February, 1968 shows a curtain of stalactites growing from the foundation ceiling beneath the Lincoln Memorial built in 1923 in Washington, D.C. Some of the stalactites had grown to five feet long in the 45 years since the memorial was built. At the evolutionary uniformitarian rate, that would indicate that the Lincoln Memorial was built about 6,000 years ago, even before the construction of the Great Pyramids of Egypt.

Figure 49. A BONDED BAT

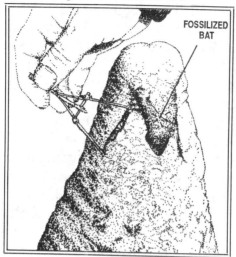

FOSSILIZED BAT

Fast-Growing 'Tites and 'Mites.

The growth rate of stalactites and stalagmites is quite slow in many caves today. But, the current rate of growth does not necessarily indicate past rates. Many factors influence growth rate. We know that in tropical areas cave formations develop much faster than those in more temperate regions. This is because of the higher annual rainfall.

In Sequoyah Caverns, located south of Chattanooga, Tennessee, at Valley Head, Alabama, there are fast-growing formations. The director of the caverns, Clark Byers, cemented a clear plastic panel in front of some stalactites in April 1977 to prevent tourists from breaking them off. In less than 10 years the stalactites had grown about 10 inches — or one inch per year.

Because of the evidence of fast-growing stalactites , we can safely conclude that the world's beautiful limestone cave formations may not have needed eons of time to form. These spectacular formations could have formed quite rapidly in just a few thousand years. This is a framework consistent with the view that they were formed during the Flood of Noah's time. A reasonable age for the limestone caverns is five thousand years. **(See fig. 50.)**

Figure 50. THE ROCK OF AGES

Chapter Nineteen

Testimony 21: Fingerprints of God

Figure 51. CREATION 'S STOPWATCH

Creation's Stopwatch.

A recent discovery within the crust of the Earth reveals another amazing testimony for a young Earth. It has sparked a fiery challenge to evolutionism's ancient Earth theory. The new evidence is called a radiohalo. It is like a stopwatch which counted and recorded the seconds it took for the creation of the Earth to occur. It gives one more powerful proof that the age of the

Earth is quite young, and that it was created by a supernatural Creator.

Radiation Leaves a Signature.

Microscopic bits of radioactive material like uranium have left their signatures in the basement rocks, or foundational rocks, of the Earth.

The basement rocks (lowest bedrock layer) of the Earth lie under the sedimentary layers of rock formed during Noah's Flood. **(See fig. 52.)** Basement granites are considered the oldest rock layers of strata formed at the beginning of creation. Evolution claims these basement rock layers were formed long before life suddenly appeared on Earth from the molten magma which took "millions" of years to cool.

All around the world this basement rock layer contains tiny microscopic stains called pieochroic halos. It has been estimated that there may be as many as 1,000,000,000,000,000 of these tiny spots.

When the radioactive uranium decayed, it gave off radiation which left a tiny sphere-shaped mark somewhat like the burn marks made by cigarettes often seen on hotel furniture.. These tiny microscopic spheres of discoloration permanently sealed inside the rock are called "radiohalos." The spots look like tiny stains with

Figure 52. BASEMENT ROCK

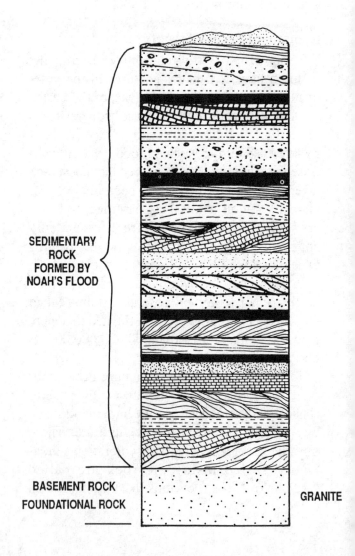

SEDIMENTARY
ROCK
FORMED BY
NOAH'S FLOOD

BASEMENT ROCK
FOUNDATIONAL ROCK

GRANITE

several rings encircling them, thus the term "halo". (See fig. 53.)

Watermarks on Bond Paper.

One amazing aspect of these tiny spots is that there is no way they could have been placed within the rock after the rock was created. They had to have been there right from the beginning. Like watermarks in fine bond paper, they couldn't have been inserted afterward; they had to be infused during the processing.

These tiny marks clearly indicate that the original process that created the rocks didn't allow any vapor, liquid or molten stage as evolutionary uniformitarianism proposes. These tiny spots may be one of the best evidences for the sudden creation of the Earth as recorded in scripture.

A study of these reveals that each ring represents a different kind of a radioactive element. Each ring is like a fingerprint that allows one to identify the element that made the ring.

For some of these rings to have formed requires:

1. They had to be formed when the rock was in a solidified state, not in a molten state.
2. They had to be formed when the rock was formed.

Figure 53. RADIOACTIVE HALO

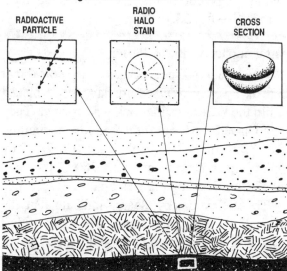

3. They had to be formed in several seconds to
    several minutes, 10 minutes maximum.

    The evidence of the halos indicates that the
basement rocks of the Earth were formed suddenly,
in a solid state and within a very short period of time.

Ship in a Bottle.

Figure 54. THE AGE-OLD MYSTERY

These radiohalos present a dilemma for the evolutionists. The puzzle is similar to a ship in a bottle. How did it get there? In order for the ship to get into the bottle, the bottle must be broken, but if the bottle is broken to get the ship inside, it cannot be put back together in its unbroken form. In this analogy, the bottle represents the granite, and the ship represents the polonium halo. How did the polonium and its resultant halos come to be in the granite?

The half-life of polonium 214 is 0.000164 seconds. In other words, this radioactive particle makes its mark in a flash. In order for the polonium to record its mark, the granite had to be completely intact and crystallized in a fraction of a second. The halo is the result of this radioactive process.

If there were cracks in the rock which would allow the radioactive bits of polonium to slip in, then we would have a logical explanation for the halos. But there are no cracks in the rock — just as there are no cracks in the bottle for the ship to be slipped through. The lack of a seam in the glass indicates two halves were not bonded together after the ship was placed inside. The only other alternative is that the ship was inserted while the glass was in a molten mass.

Maybe the granite was still in a molten form at the time the polonium entered into the rock. However, this is impossible: if the granite was in the molten state necessary to allow the polonium entrance, no halo could form. By the time the molten granite would have cooled and solidified, the polonium halo would not form a perfectly symmetrical halo; it would have totally assimilated into the molten rock. The ship could not have been inserted while the glass was in a molten mass; the ship would be charred from the heat of the glass. The secret of the ship is that it is inserted in tiny pieces through the opening, and then painstakingly assembled bit by bit. This is a very lengthy and time-consuming procedure. However, there is no "technique" that will insert the bits of radioactive material into the molten rock once it becomes hard. And there is no technique that would allow the polonium halo "ship" to escape imperfection if the rock was in a molten state when the radioactive polonium particle entered.

The Problem.

If the granite is hardened, the radioactive polonium particle cannot enter into the rock; and if the granite is not hardened, no halo can form.

The Solution.

The time in which the molten granite was penetrable before it hardened was extremely brief. One kind of halo forms in less than ten minutes, and another in just a few seconds. This means that the evolutionary model for the time required for the cooling and solidification of the granite — millions and millions of years — is totally erroneous. Otherwise the halos could never have formed in the shape in which they are found. The only alternative is that these halos were formed during creation when the granite rock and radioactive particles were simultaneously created. The Bible reveals that God created by "fiat," meaning instantly and out of nothing. No one thus far has come up with any other alternative solution to account for the halos.

The Formation of Coal.

Radiohalos exist in coal formations. Evolutionism has taught that coal was formed millions of years ago; however, these radiohalos tell us a different story. As previously discussed, these halos could not form until after the coal had begun to form. Thus, at the time of the formation of the coal, tiny radioactive bits of uranium were locked into the coal and the halos formed. The precise time necessary for the formation of coal can be measured. Each halo is like a stopwatch that begins counting when the coal begins to form and stops when it solidifies. This process reveals that coal formations are only a few thousand years old, and that their formation was very rapid. The Genesis Flood could easily account for such rapid formation.

Robert Gentry's Research.

Robert Gentry is one of the men who has done immense research on radiohalos in rocks. Gentry's more than 20 years of work and observation qualify him as one of the world's leading authorities on radiohalos. All during his research he has submitted his results to the evolutionary scientific community for review. His work has been published in such prestigious scientific journals as *Science, Nature,* and *Physics Today.*

Radiohalos indicate that the basic evolutionary premise for Earth history is wrong. Gentry says that rocks known as pre-cambrian granites (the basement or foundation rocks of the Earth) were created almost instantly as a part of the creation event recorded in Genesis 1:1 and not as a result of evolutionism. Gentry also points out that the "big bang" version of the creation of the sun and the Earth is without any scientific basis.

Gentry concludes that scientific evidence establishes that the age of the Earth's oldest rocks cannot be more than a few thousand years.

Thus far, Gentry's work has not been refuted. In 1984 the U.S. National Academy of Sciences published a booklet which heavily criticized the biblical perspective of creation. Gentry took exception, and made a public challenge to the Academy.

In 1986, Gentry wrote to the Academy and requested any evolutionary studies which refuted his results. None came. Next he invited the Academy's president and any other evolutionists to come and attend a scientific presentation of his work at the international conference in Pittsburgh in 1986. They were asked to bring any evidence which they believed invalidated his scientific research. No one came or even responded until eight months later when the president of the National Academy of Sciences merely presented his belief that evolutionism was true.

Later, another invitation to refute Gentry's work was made to the University of Tennessee but again no one from the Academy turned up. The evolutionary community continues to respond to Gentry's conclusions with scorn and with typical emotional heavy-handedness. They have made certain that Gentry's research grant was cut off by the National Science Foundation and his visiting status terminated. Those under the delusion of evolutionism seek to destroy anything or anyone that would bring them face to face with the God of the universe.[12]

Creator's Fingerprint.

There is hardly a more graphic evidence for biblical creation than the radiohalos. It is as if the Creator left His signature disbursed among the rocks, attesting to a sudden creation. No other reasonable explanation has been presented by the evolutionary community in spite of all the scientific knowledge.

Though the Bible neither stands nor falls on the accuracy of Gentry's work, his research certainly presents a challenge to basic evolutionary premises.

---

12 A short technical summary of this study can be found in *The Creator's Signature* by William Overn, printed by the Bible Science Association, Minneapolis, MN 55406

PART IV
YOUNG UNIVERSE CLOCKS

Chapter Twenty

Testimonies of Young Universe Clocks

The evidence in support of a young universe has grown rapidly in recent years as a result of the advances both in space exploration and the field of astronomy. Nevertheless, old ideas die hard, and evolutionism, with its requirement of billions of years of cosmic history, must maintain its position or its "Tower of Babylon" will come tumbling down. Millions of tax dollars and untold hours of scientific brainpower are being wasted in an attempt to keep the evolutionary tower from crumbling.

About 2,000 years before Christ, another civilization attempted to erect a tower. The Tower of Babel was to be a monument of man's ability to reach into the heavens. That endeavor ended in judgment. Today, some 2,000 years after the birth of Christ, man once again is erect-

Figure 55. SPACE EXPLORATION

© *CB* 1993

ing a tower to the heavens, one that is rooted in an anti-God system. No doubt judgment awaits those who are putting their trust in such an edifice to unite and save man.

Part of that tower erected by man is the U.S. space program. In 1986 the Discovery Space Shuttle disaster occurred. On this special day, children across the nation were watching TV monitors in their classrooms. This historic flight was to carry its first school teacher into space. Just seconds after lift-off an explosion occurred aboard the shuttle, killing the entire crew. The disaster was a clear indication as to the futility in trusting space exploration as the savior of mankind.

In 1964, God was officially removed from the U.S. public school system by the Supreme Court. Interestingly, it was shortly after this that the government began to invest billions of dollars into space research.

In 1990, the Hubble Space Telescope costing 1.6 billion tax dollars was sent into space to help answer some disturbing questions. These questions were raised due to new information which conflicts drastically with evolutionism. However, because of the weight the evolutionary theory carries in the minds of many, it still has an enormous stronghold over them.

In this section we will look at several clocks which have recently been discovered as a result of the space program. These clocks testify to a recent and young creation.

Chapter Twenty-One

Testimony 22: Tales of Comets' Tails

Figure 56. COMET CLOCKS

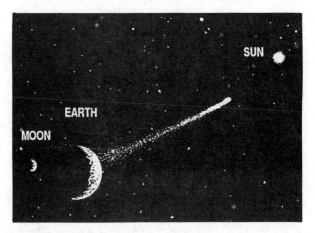

A Tail of a Comet.

When we picture a comet, we naturally see it with a long visible tail. But the fact is, through most of each orbital period no tail is visible. It is only when a comet approaches close to the sun that the tail appears.

The tail of a comet is comprised of material that is being burned off the body of the comet. As comets make their circuits around the sun, pieces are blown off by the powerful solar wind coming from the sun. On every pass by the sun, more of the comet's matter is blasted from its surface to become part of its tail. **(See fig. 57.)**

This loss of material of comets with each passage by the sun is the basis for a very important clock. The solar janitor (our sun, as discussed earlier) is not only sweeping the solar system clean of tiny bits of material, but also of comets by burning off a substantial portion of their mass during each close approach to it.

Comets, then, eventually disintegrate completely. Over the centuries the destruction of many comets has been observed and recorded. There have been ten recorded observations of comet destruction in this century. Sometimes comets break up into smaller pieces, and sometimes they disappear entirely during their close approach to the sun.

A perplexing problem arises here for evolutionists. The average life span for comets is only 1,500 to 10,000 years. Measuring the observable rate of comet disintegration, scientists realize that it would take only 10,000 years to rid our solar system of all its comets. This

Figure 57. COMET CLUTTER

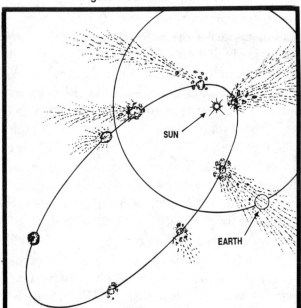

means that if the solar system were even as old as one-half million years, there would be no comets left in it. Yet astronomers tell us that there are up to five million comets still orbiting in our solar system.

A Tale of a Comet.

Unwilling to admit the possibility that this clock might indicate that the comets — as well as the solar system itself — were created less than 10,000 years ago, evolutionists are forced to dodge the issue by devising alternative theories. The evolutionary scientists' stubborn refusal to accept the truth leaves them open to deception. In their efforts to provide options viable in their own eyes, they sometimes drift off into the realm of the fantastic and the improbable. One of their theories suggests that there is a huge nest of comets in the outer reaches of the solar system. Every once in awhile some cosmic disturbance supposedly kicks some of these out of the nest. Has anyone ever seen this nest? Well, no; because it lies just outside of the reach of our most powerful telescopes, we are told. But such ridiculous explanations must be considered if one insists upon avoiding the glaringly obvious conclusion that the planets and the comets just haven't been in existence very long.

Another incredible theory seems more like science fiction than reasonable scientific conjecture. This notion suggests that comets are belched out by erupting volcanoes, most probably on Jupiter, and are expelled into orbit. However, not only is there no known planetary mechanism to impart the force needed to expel a comet into orbit, but if there were such, it is estimated it would need 370-miles-per-second speed to put it into orbit around the sun.

Traveling at this speed would burn up and vaporize the comet before it ever left the atmosphere of its mother planet.

Obviously, the apparent recent origin of comets leads to the conclusion that the age of the comets, and hence the solar system, is quite young — several thousand years at most. Here we have another testimony in favor of a recent creation.

Chapter Twenty-Two

Testimony 23: Icy Hot Planets

Figure 58. JUPITER'S JOLT

Evolutionary scientists are once again scrambling in an attempt to try to resolve the implications of a recent discovery made by the Voyager Spacecraft. A relatively small moon of

Jupiter, Io, has something on it which it isn't suppose to have (according to evolutionism) — hot volcanoes. **(See fig. 59)** The evolutionists' dilemma can be illustrated in the following example.

Imagine you are hiking in the Rocky Mountains in Colorado in a remote area not often visited by man. You are heading towards a secluded cabin high up on the side of a mountain near the timberline. The cabin is owned by a friend of yours, and he has loaned it to you for a week. He advised you that it may not be in the best of condition because there hasn't been anyone in it for over a year. After arriving and unlocking the door, you enter. As you look around, you notice that there are some smoldering coals in the fireplace. Although there isn't anyone around now, it is evident that someone was recently in the cabin. Your friend apparently was mistaken about no one using the cabin in over a year because the evidence is quite clear that someone has been there very recently.

Some years back, NASA made a similar discovery. In 1979, the Voyager Space Probe explored the planet Jupiter. Among the spectacular pictures transmitted back to Earth was a most incredible scene — an erupting volcano on Io, one of Jupiter's moons. Voyager's cameras

Figure 59. IO'S ENIGMA

caught the eruption as it was passing by. This relatively small moon was described by *National Geographic* as the most volcanic body yet discovered in the entire solar system.

Io, 200°F Below 0.

What was amazing about the eruption was that it was totally unexpected by NASA's evolutionary scientists. In their view, the moons of Jupiter were formed at the same time as the planet itself, and they believe it came into existence about 4½ billion years ago. Therefore small bodies such as the moon Io should have lost their interior heat and their ability to generate volcanic activity. Evolutionists realize that there is no way a small body such as Io could possibly survive the -200°F temperatures beyond 10-50 thousand years, and certainly not 4½ billion years, without becoming a frozen chunk of ice. In their eyes, Io should long ago have become cold and inactive because of its supposed 4.5-billion-year age. The hot flowing lava spewing out of Io's surface 150 miles into space is one of the strongest evidences yet of a young solar system.

Life Magazine Comments.

The fact that Io is still hot and active in its interior delivers a forceful message. Here is a quote from a report that appeared in *Life* magazine (May 1979) following the Voyager mission:

> The big surprise of the Voyager mission was Io, one of Jupiter's inner moons. Instead of being cold, dead and otherwise moonlike, Io proved to be literally bubbling with volcanoes. Voyager's cameras witnessed one eruption on the moon's rim ... that spewed fire and brimstone more than 100 miles into space.... Earth was hitherto considered the only geologically active body in the solar system, but Io was found to be even more violent.

How can a moon of Jupiter be so old and still be so hot and active? The same way a fire can burn for a year. It can't. The solution, however simple, is unthinkable to evolutionists. Maybe Io, just like the smoldering fire in the cabin fireplace, is not so old after all. Here is another clock within our universe which testifies to a young creation.

Maintaining a Sacred Belief.

Many evolutionists, unwilling to accept the obvious, are trying to come up with theories to explain how Io can still be hot. One theory postulates that Jupiter's gravity is so strong it affects its moons — that it acts like a heat pump which is "pumping" energy to the moons to produce heat. Of course there is no known physical evidence or even a law of physics that can account for such a hypothesis as "gravitational heat pumping."

Evolutionists are not concerned with the evidence, but with maintaining their sacred belief that the age of the solar system is 4½ billion years. Keep in mind that the question evolutionists ask is not how old is the universe, but how is the universe old? They realize that if the universe is not old, evolutionism is not possible.

Chapter Twenty-Three

Testimonies 24-25:
Rings and More Hot Things

Figure 60.TEXAS-SIZED ICE RINK

SATURN

Testimony 24: Saturn's Rings.

Suppose you were on your way to pick up a

show horse you'd just inherited. You have been told that it is a beautiful, well-trained stallion which has won numerous awards for its performance and appearance. After arriving at the training facility your horse is brought out to you — kicking, rearing, snorting and neighing fiercely. It is very apparent that something is wrong. Although it is a lovely stallion, it is obvious that it is very young and untrained. Someone has made a mistake.

Likewise, it appears there has been an error regarding the age of Saturn's rings. Instead of being found in an orderly and uniform orbit, Voyager space probes discovered them to be in a state of turbulence and instability.

Evolutionists were totally astonished by their disorderly state. Rings that supposedly have existed for 4½ billion years should be in a very stable condition. The chunks of ice which make up the rings should have stabilized long ago to form a consistent and uniform pattern surrounding the planet.

The photographic data that Voyager sent back revealed instability and bizarre physical conditions that violate basic laws of physics — *if* the rings are truly 4.5 billion years old. Scientists know that there is no way the rings could have remained in such a state of instability for more than 10-50 thousand years, and certainly not millions or billions of years, especially since they are composed of billions of individual particles all revolving around Saturn at different speeds. *National Geographic* confesses:

> The rings are so dynamic that some scientists are now questioning the long-held belief that the rings are as old as the (supposed age of the) solar system.[13]

If, however, Saturn's rings are only a few thousand years old, their present status presents no difficulty with the known physical laws. It is the same as with embers in one's fireplace: if they smolder for a day or so, they do not present any contradictions to known physical laws; however, if they are believed to have been smoldering for a year, then there is a problem.

Testimony 25: Ringed Hot Planet.

As Voyager flew past Neptune, more startling facts were revealed. *U.S. News and World Report* stated:

> Researchers ... announced several key discoveries including unexpected turbulent weather systems and rings con-

---

13 *National Geographic*, Jan. 85, pg. 48.

taining odd clumps of debris held together by some as yet unknown mechanism ... Neptune's pink-tinted moon, Triton, generated the most astonishing news.[14]

What was this astonishing news? Lawrence Sodeblom of the U.S. Geological Survey said that the data seems to reveal that there are volcanoes on Triton which have erupted within the last several hundred years. This caused quite a great stir in the evolutionary community, which is not willing to give up their ancient solar system hypothesis. In the same report we read, "One problem with Sodeblom's idea is where the energy is coming from to drive such a system." In other words, since Triton is such an enormous distance from the sun, the temperature is less than -300°F.

Sky & Telescope said that "some unknown source of heat would be required to melt the ice."[15] If one assumes Triton is 4½ billion years old, there must be an unknown heat source to melt the ice that would otherwise accumulate. Such a relatively small body in freezing temperatures should long ago have been frozen solid. This is the same problem that was encountered

14 *U.S. News & World Report*, Sept. 11, 1989, p.60
15 *Sky & Telescope*, Vol. 79, No. 2, p. 155

with Jupiter's moon Io, except that Triton is about 100 degrees colder than Io. To put it simply, if someone opened up your freezer and found a cup of hot coffee, it would be pretty hard to convince your friends that it had been there for a whole year.

Photographs showed that Triton had volcanic plumes rising more than five miles above the surface and drifting more than 80 miles downwind. Four volcanic plumes were spotted, and *Sky & Telescope* reported:

> Triton's enigmatic surface plays host to a number of dynamic processes that are not yet fully understood ... at least a billion years of geologic record appears to be missing.[16]

What is missing isn't a billion years of geologic record, but a heart willing to accept the evidence which testifies to a recent creation — one that harmonizes with a biblical perspective.

---

[16] Ibid., p. 154, February 1990

Chapter Twenty-Four

Testimonies 26 & 27:Strange Stories in the Stars

Figure 61. SUPER GIANTS

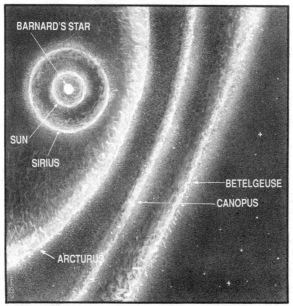

Testimony 26: "B" & "O" Barn Burners.

B & O Barn Burners do not only identify the

farmer whose livelihood is raising swine, but B & O also identifies objects within the heavens which radiate solar energy unlike anything one can imagine.

There are sights in the heavens that are stranger than science fiction and more amazing than anything known to man. Such wonders display the glory of God and His eternal powers.

Astronomers have established a scale by which the amount of energy stars give off is measured. Letters are designated to each star type. Some stars are smaller and much cooler than our sun. Our sun is labeled a "G" type, meaning it is an average star with a surface temperature of nearly 10,000°F. (**See fig. 62.**)

Some stars are much hotter and larger than our sun. These are monstrous energy burners, with diameters 10,000 times that of our sun and having temperatures of over 90,000° F. They are labeled "B" and "O" types. These "B" and "O" stars radiate more than 100,000 times the energy of our sun. Calculating backward, the entire universe would have been filled with the mass of these stars just a few thousand years ago — not billions or even millions. Here again we see evidence for a young universe and not the mythological notion of billions of years.

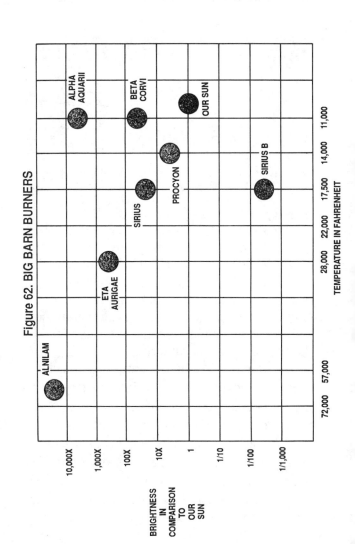

Figure 62. BIG BARN BURNERS

Testimony 27: The Mystery of Sirius B.

Figure 63. A WHITE DWARF

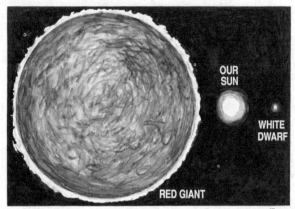

OUR
SUN

WHITE
DWARF

RED GIANT

In 1978 at Louisiana State University in Baton Rouge, a symposium with top scientists was held to discuss the issue of time and the age of the Earth and cosmos. Certain problems and contradictions in the current evolutionary conception of an ancient universe were explored by the scientists at this gathering.

Among the fascinating topics discussed was a puzzle known as "The Sirius Mystery." This mystery centers on a star named Sirius B, which is a type of star referred to as a "white dwarf." A white dwarf star is one which has exhausted its energy and shrunk to the size of our Earth. The problem stems from the fact that throughout history astronomers have been well-acquainted with Sirius B. However, the ancient astronomers described Sirius as a red star rather than a white one. A red star is a giant one about 100 times the present size of our sun, and it appears red. Ancient astronomers recorded the following:

1. Egyptian hieroglyphs from 2,000 B.C. described Sirius as red.

2. Cicero (Roman philosopher-1st century B.C.), writing in 50 B.C., stated that Sirius was red.

3. Seneca (Roman statesman-1st century B.C.) described Sirius as being more red than Mars, which he in turn described as more red than Jupiter.

4. The famous early astronomer Ptolemy in A.D. 150 listed Sirius as one of six red stars.

Modern astronomers are forced to accept the idea that within historical times Sirius B was transformed from a red giant to a white dwarf star. What is the problem with that? According to present conceptions of thermonuclear star radiation, it should take at least 100,000 years for a red giant star to collapse into a white dwarf star. Something is obviously wrong with the present conception of stars. Maybe the ancients' eyes were color blind. Or maybe the meaning of the words they used have changed since they recorded their observations. Or just maybe the stars aren't as old as evolutionism claims and they burn out much faster than evolutionism declares. Once again, it is obvious that the evolutionists' problem isn't with time, but rather with the One who rules time.

Chapter Twenty-Five

Testimony 28: Galaxy Clusters

During the days when Tom Landry coached the Dallas Cowboys, occasionally I would have an opportunity to attend one of their football games. On special occasions, during the halftime festivities, thousands of helium-filled balloons would be released as a net was pulled away. **(See fig. 64.)** The balloons would immediately begin their upward drift into the sky through the big hole in the top of the semi-covered Texas stadium. As they sailed upward, they constituted a kind of clock: at the start they were all tightly clustered together, but as they ascended, the cluster gradually broke up. After a while there were hundreds of balloons, each going its own way, producing a vast field of balloons without any clusters. This same phenomenon can be seen in the heavenlies, except for one thing: there are still clusters of galaxies — after 20 billion years? **(See fig. 65.)**

Figure 64. COWBOY HOOPLA

Outside our solar system in the galaxies beyond, a number of observations don't fit with the idea of an ancient universe. The relative motions of stars can be plotted and their relative speeds measured. What is puzzling about some star clusters is that the stars in these groups are racing away from each other at great speeds and yet are still relatively close to each other. If they had been flying apart for billions of years, they would be nowhere near each other.

In the heavens there is a condition much like our balloon illustration. Every galaxy consists of a cluster of millions and millions of stars. And

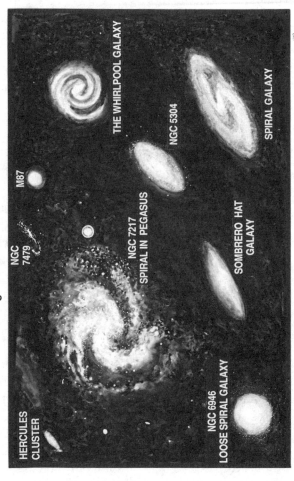

Figure 65. GALAXY CLUSTERS

THE WHIRLPOOL GALAXY

SPIRAL GALAXY

NGC 5304

M87

NGC 7479

NGC 7217
SPIRAL IN PEGASUS

SOMBRERO HAT
GALAXY

HERCULES
CLUSTER

NGC 6946
LOOSE SPIRAL GALAXY

© CB 1993

then there are clusters of galaxies. These galaxy clusters are held together by gravitational fields. But as time passes, the gravitational fields decay and weaken. As a result, the galaxies break up — just as the balloons released from the net did. Now what is most disturbing from an evolutionary point of view is the fact that calculations indicate that the amount of time needed for "breakup" or dissipation of the galaxy clusters is at most only two to four million years. This, of course, indicates that the universe cannot be anywhere near the 10 to 20 billion years required by the theory of evolutionism. If evolutionists were correct, and galaxy clusters had been around for ten to twenty billion years, then many galaxy clusters should have dissipated into fields of individual galaxies — just as the cluster became a field of balloons spread out across the Dallas sky. The clusters of galaxies are, in fact, breaking up; but they are still in clusters because they have not existed long enough to dissipate. In their present stage of breakup, even using evolutionistic methods of calculating, the absolute maximum age for most clusters is two to four million years. The small clusters have breakup times indicating a maximum age of only a few thousand years. It is apparent that the age of the universe is only several thousand years just as the Bible affirms. The field of astronomy continues to discover clocks which put the age of the universe on the side of youth rather than antiquity.

PART V
GRANDFATHER TIME

Chapter Twenty-Six

Grandfather Time: The Hero or Villain of the Plot

Evolutionists disagree among themselves on almost every aspect of evolutionism. They argue about how life occurred and when and where it occurred. Did it happen on Earth or in space? Was the rate of development slow or rapid? However, there is one aspect which is essential to their plot to which all of Darwin's disciples unanimously agree, and that is the matter of time.

Unless there is sufficient time, evolutionism doesn't have a ghost of a chance to work. Dr. Robert Jastrow, one of the world's foremost evolutionary scientists, expressed it by saying, "The key to Darwin's explanation is time, and the passage of many centuries." (*Until the Sun Dies*, Robert Jastrow, Warner Books, 1980, New York, p. 112).

Another well-known evolutionary scholar, Dr. George Wald, professor at Harvard University, expressed the importance of time in an article on the origin of life:

> The important point is that since the origin of life belongs in the category of 'at-least-once' phenomena, time is on its side. However improbable we regard this event, or any of the steps it involves, given enough time, it will almost certainly happen at least once. And for life as we know it, with its capability for growth and reproduction, once may be enough. Time is the hero of the plot. The time with which we have to deal here is on the order of 2 billion years. What we regard as impossible on the basis of human experience is meaningless here. Given so much time, the impossible becomes possible, the possible becomes probable, and the probable becomes virtually certain. One has only to wait, time itself performs the miracles.[17]

Time is the all-essential ingredient to the hodgepodge 20th century adult fairy tale.

---

[17] "The Origin of Life," *Scientific American*, Aug. 1954, pp. 45-54).

Without time, the hero quickly becomes the villain and the tale quickly ends with the evolutionist grasping for straws as he goes under for the last time.

So important is time to their theory that the evolutionary community finds it necessary to double the approximate age of the Earth every 20 years. During the 1800s evolutionists estimated the age of the Earth to be between 3 million to 1.6 billion years. However, it soon became apparent that the theory of evolutionism could not possibly work. So evolutionists were compelled to assume longer and longer periods of time for the evolutionary history of the Earth. Over the past century, the estimated age of the Earth has doubled approximately every 20 years.

It is absolutely amazing to see how educated men of science can ascribe to the bankrupt system of evolutionism. But then again ego will lead to deception of even the wisest. Mark Twain, though he was no supporter of the Bible, had enough insight to see the nonsense of evolutionism during his day. He poked fun at evolutionists' hero, Time, in his book, *Life on the Mississippi*:

> In the space of one hundred and seventy-six years the Lower

Mississippi has shortened itself two hundred and forty-two miles. That is an average of a trifle over one mile and a third per year. Therefore, any calm person, who is not blind or idiotic, can see that in the Old Oolitic Silurian Period, just a million years ago next November, the Lower Mississippi River was upward of one million three hundred thousand miles long, and stuck out over the Gulf of Mexico like a fishing rod. And by the same token any person can see that seven hundred and forty-two years from now the Lower Mississippi will be only a mile and three quarters long, and Cairo and New Orleans will have joined their streets together, and be plodding comfortably along under a single mayor and a mutual board of aldermen. There is something fascinating about science. One gets such wholesale returns of conjecture out of such trifling investment of fact.

In other words, Mr. Twain says its amazing how one who has little or no evidence can come up with such incredulous conclusions. Such notions might be as sensible as the Queen's comments to Alice in Lewis Carroll's *Alice in Wonderland:*

> Alice laughed, 'There's no use trying,'
> she said, 'One can't believe impossi-
> ble things.' 'I dare say you haven't had
> much practice,' said the Queen. 'When
> I was your age I did it for half an hour
> a day. Why sometimes I've believed as
> many as six impossible things before
> breakfast.'

It seems that the Queen had evolutionism in mind when it comes to believing the impossible.

Chapter Twenty-Seven

Testimony 29: Time — Savior or Destroyer of Evolutionism

Anything is Possible — Or is it?

The mysteries of the Earth that cast doubt on scientists' present theories can't be dissolved by the notion that "given enough time, anything could have happened."

Evolutionism teaches that life began 2½ to 3½ billion years ago with an unlikely accident, and gradually developed through a series of improbable coincidences in a random, unplanned process. In time, through natural selection, the one cell split and became two, and so on, until man arrived on the scene. **(See fig. 66)**

Question: Is the amount of time imagined by evolutionists long enough to have caused the first one-celled creature to evolve (not to mention to explain how the first cell suddenly appeared in the first place) and change into all the life forms up to and including man?

Figure 66. THE FAMILY ZOO

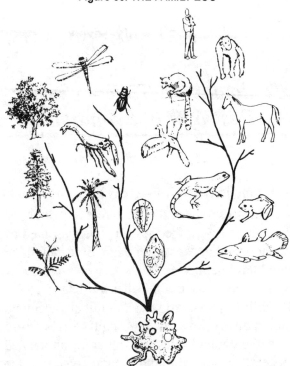

Research at M.I.T.

How realistic is this notion that given enough time, a one-celled creature evolved into man? Some years ago, I went to hear Harry Conn, chairman of the Whitney Corporation, a large engineering company on the New York Stock Exchange. According to him, the computers at the Massachusetts Institute of Technology tell us the evolutionary theory is not realistic at all. The computers calculated that if changes took place every second (although evolutionists tell us that many changes needed thousands of years), there still wouldn't be enough time for a single cell (**see fig. 67**) to have changed into complex multicellular organisms like man (**see fig. 68**) in 10 billion years. This is more than twice as much time given for the age of the Earth by evolutionists, and more than four times the amount of time given since life supposedly "suddenly" appeared.

Time is not the savior of evolutionism; it is the destroyer. The more time, the less chance there is for order and complexity to exist. Design and complexity cannot increase over time because of the Second Law of Thermodynamics. This law of physics is known in biblical terms as the law of decay and death — the result of the curse. Only a Supreme Intelligence could possibly be the cause of complex living organisms such as man coming into being in the short time span observed for the age of the universe.

Figure 67. THE SUPER CELL

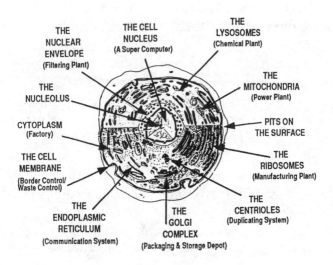

Figure 68. SUPER MAN

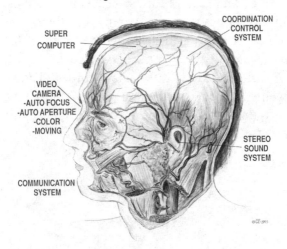

Figure 68. SUPER MAN (cont.)

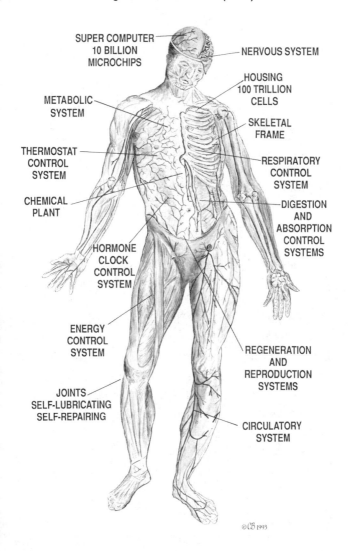

SUPER COMPUTER
10 BILLION
MICROCHIPS

NERVOUS SYSTEM

HOUSING
100 TRILLION
CELLS

METABOLIC
SYSTEM

SKELETAL
FRAME

THERMOSTAT
CONTROL
SYSTEM

RESPIRATORY
CONTROL
SYSTEM

CHEMICAL
PLANT

DIGESTION
AND
ABSORPTION
CONTROL
SYSTEMS

HORMONE
CLOCK
CONTROL
SYSTEM

ENERGY
CONTROL
SYSTEM

REGENERATION
AND
REPRODUCTION
SYSTEMS

JOINTS
SELF-LUBRICATING
SELF-REPAIRING

CIRCULATORY
SYSTEM

© CB 1993

Chapter Twenty-Eight

Testimony 30: Where Are All the People?

Population Growth Statistics.

One of the most revealing testimonies for a young Earth is a clock connected with the growth of Earth's population down through time. If man has been on Earth for a million years, why is the population explosion only recently becoming a problem? In A.D. 1650 there were only 400 million people on the Earth. By the 1800s, the Earth's population had risen to 850 million; and today there are more than 5 *billion*. **(See fig. 69.)**

Does the present-day population correspond with the belief that man has been on Earth for a million years? Calculating from a million years ago, what should the Earth's population be today? How much land area would be needed to hold a million-year population growth? Evolution says nothing about the general animal

Figure 69. POPULATION EXPLOSION

populace. It would seem that the animal population should be even greater if life has existed on Planet Earth for more than a milliion years. Yet we find many animals have become extinct.

Annual Increase.

Today the average family worldwide has 3.6 children and the annual population increases only by 2%. Even if we were to take a more conservative approach in our calculations and reduce these figures from 3.6 to 2.5 children per family and 2% to ½% annual population increase, the present population would have been developed from a single family in only 4,000 years. This reduction in percentages is a fourth of the present rate of growth and would allow for the periods in which there was no growth due to famines, plagues and wars with which history is replete.

What does the evolutionary framework have to offer in this regard? First of all, the supposed million-year history of man would mean that there should have been an incredible 25,000 generations at 40 years each. Now if we would take the same conservative figures previously used (½% annual increase and 2.5 children per family), and multiply it by 25,000 consecutive generations we would have a staggering number:

10^{2100}. Such a number would be represented by the number 1 followed by 2,100 zeros and look like this:

10000000000000000000000000000000000
00000000000000000000000000000000000
00000000000000000000000000000000000
00000000000000000000000000000000000
00000000000000000000000000000000000
00000000000000000000000000000000000
00000000000000000000000000000000000
00000000000000000000000000000000000
00000000000000000000000000000000000
00000000000000000000000000000000000
00000000000000000000000000000000000
00000000000000000000000000000000000
00000000000000000000000000000000000
00000000000000000000000000000000000
00000000000000000000000000000000000
00000000000000000000000000000000000
00000000000000000000000000000000000
00000000000000000000000000000000000
00000000000000000000000000000000000
00000000000000000000000000000000000
00000000000000000000000000000000000
00000000000000000000000000000000000
00000000000000000000000000000000000
00000000000000000000000000000000000
00000000000000000000000000000000000
00000000000000000000000000000000000

OOOOOOOOOOOOOOOOOOOOOOOOOOOOOOOOOOOOOO
OOOOOOOOOOOOOOOOOOOOOOOOOOOOOOOOOOOOOO
OOOOOOOOOOOOOOOOOOOOOOOOOOOOOOOOOOOOOO
OOOOOOOOOOOOOOOOOOOOOOOOOOOOOOOOOOOOOO
OOOOOOOOOOOOOOOOOOOOOOOOOOOOOOOOOOOOOO
OOOOOOOOOOOOOOOOOOOOOOOOOOOOOOOOOOOOOO
OOOOOOOOOOOOOOOOOOOOOOOOOOOOOOOOOOOOOO
OOOOOOOOOOOOOOOOOOOOOOOOOOOOOOOOOOOOOO
OOOOOOOOOOOOOOOOOOOOOOOOOOOOOOOOOOOOOO
OOOOOOOOOOOOOOOOOOOOOOOOOOOOOOOOOOOOOO
OOOOOOOOOOOOOOOOOOOOOOOOOOOOOOOOOOOOOO
OOOOOOOOOOOOOOOOOOOOOOOOOOOOOOOOOOOOOO
OOOOOOOOOOOOOOOOOOOOOOOOOOOOOOOOOOOOOO
OOOOOOOOOOOOOOOOOOOOOOOOOOOOOOOOOOOOOO
OOOOOOOOOOOOOOOOOOOOOOOOOOOOOOOOOOOOOO
OOOOOOOOOOOOOOOOOOOOOOOOOOOOOOOOOOOOOO
OOOOOOOOOOOOOOOOOOOOOOOOOOOOOOOOOOOOOO
OOOOOOOOOOOOOOOOOOOOOOOOOOOOOOOOOOOOOO
OOOOOOOOOOOOOOOOOOOOOOOOOOOOOOOOOOOOOO
OOOOOOOOOOOOOOOOOOOOOOOOOOOOOOOOOOOOOO
OOOOOOOOOOOOOOOOOOOOOOOOOOOOOOOOOOOOOO
OOOOOOOOOOOOOOOOOOOOOOOOOOOOOOOOOOOOOO
OOOOOOOOOOOOOOOOOOOOOOOOOOOOOOOOOOOOOO
OOOOOOOOOOOOOOOOOOOOOOOOOOOOOOOOOOOOOO
OOOOOOOOOOOOOOOOOOOOOOOOOOOOOOOOOOOOOO
OOOOOOOOOOOOOOOOOOOOOOOOOOOOOOOOOOOOOO
OOOOOOOOOOOOOOOOOOOOOOOOOOOOOOOOOOOOOO
OOOOOOOOOOOOOOOOOOOOOOOOOOOOOOOOOOOOOO
OOOOOOOOOOOOOOOOOOOOOOOOOOOOOOOOOOOOOO
OOOOOOOOOOOOOOOOOOOOOOOOOOOOOOOOOOOOOO

000000000000000000000000000000000000000
000000000000000000000000000000000000000
000000000000000000000000000000000000000
00000000000000000000000000000000.

Evolutionary Madness.

What does this number mean in practical terms? Not only all the Earth would be filled with people, including the oceans, but people would be stacked on top of each other past the moon, past the edge of our solar system, filling the known universe, which extends out to a distance of 10 billion light years!

But there is a problem. The whole known universe is filled with people, but you have only used up 10^{80} power. And 10^{80} is a far cry from 10^{2100}. Obviously, such a mega-number is ridiculous since the entire universe could be filled up with tiny electrons numbering only 10^{130}. The evolutionary model is nothing less than incomprehensible madness.

The Record of the Jewish People.

Applying the same formula used above to the Jewish people from Abraham forward, we can determine the approximate number of Jewish people actually living today.

Professor Harold Armstrong of Queen's University in Canada says statisticians have determined that at the present rate of growth, the human population will double about every 150 years. In the past, before advances of medicine, things such as war and disease claimed people's lives at a much younger age. So it took longer for the population to double.

Despite the Crusades, the Inquisition and the World War II Holocaust, the world's Jewish population has increased from the eight persons of around 1950 B.C. to the approximately 18 million of today. This means their population has doubled every 175 years.

By applying this 175-year figure to the entire world population today and calculating backward, we arrive at a "starting point" for the human race of only about 4,800 years ago ... close to the time of the Genesis Flood.

Assuming that man's existence began only 500,000 years ago (actually evolutionism suggests one million years and more), then the world's population has only doubled on an average of every 16,667 years to reach its current level. To even consider this figure is wishful thinking and is plainly foolish.

Where Are the Bones?

There is more to add to the evolutionary dilemma. If evolutionary history is correct, where are all the fossil remains of the supposed billions of people who would have lived and died on this planet?

Question: Even if a million years of man's history produced only the present population of approximately five billion people, at least 3 trillion people would have lived and died in that time. That's at least two dozen graves for every acre on Earth. So where are all the human bones?

Let's assume, for the sake of argument, that only twenty billion Homo sapiens (not "apemen") have lived and died over the million-year period? Why are there so few fossils to account for their numbers? Supposedly dinosaurs existed millions of years before man appeared, but not in the same numbers as man. Fossils of dinosaurs are found constantly. One would expect to find many human fossils. But this is not the case. When a human fossil is found, it is greatly heralded by the media and scientific community as a monumental discovery.

The facts line up directly with the biblical model. The evidence acknowledges that human culture began less than 5,000 years ago — the point of the global Flood.

> So God said to Noah, "I am going to
> put an end to all people, for the earth
> is filled with violence because of
> them. I am surely going to destroy
> both them and the earth" (Gen. 6:13).

Assuming that a generation is 43 years, and that an average family has 2.5 children, it would take only 100 generations from Noah to produce a world population of 4.6 billion persons, which is very close to the 5+ billion actually living on Earth today.

The observable growth rate of human population on Planet Earth fits much more naturally in a creation/global Flood framework than in an evolutionary concept. Once again we find that the Word of God provides a reasonable record that agrees with the observable evidence. **(See fig. 70.)**

Figure 70. POPULATION GRAPH

A LOOK AT THE STATISTICS

BEGINNING
1 MILLION YEARS AGO
MR. & MRS. ZINJANTHROPUS
WOULD HAVE
10^{2100}
DESCENDANTS LIVNG
ON PLANET EARTH TODAY

BEGINNING
4700 YEARS AGO
MR. & MRS. NOAH
WOULD HAVE
4.8 BILLION
DESCENDANTS LIVING
ON PLANET EARTH TODAY

BEGINNING WITH
ABRAHAM AND SARAH
THERE WOULD BE
ABOUT 18 MILLION
JEWISH PEOPLE
LIVING TODAY

Chapter Twenty-Nine

Time and Eternity

Not Limited by Time.

Let us consider time in light of eternity. The Bible reveals that God is all-powerful, all-knowing and all-present. So if God is not limited in space, then He isn't limited in time either.

If to God every point in space is here, then every moment of time is now. In other words, God is capable of seeing every part of His creation as well as every act every human being is doing. Nothing goes unnoticed by His all-seeing eyes.

> The eyes of the LORD are everywhere, keeping watch on the wicked and the good (Prov. 15:3).

> Nothing in all creation is hidden from God's sight. Everything is uncovered and laid bare before the eyes of him to

whom we must give account (Heb. 4:13).

Likewise, God is all-knowing; He knows every thought every person is thinking everywhere in the world. Nothing is hidden from His presence. Finally, nothing is forgotten unless God chooses to forget it.

The Past is Not Past.

Man likes to think the past is gone, dead and buried. But this is not true; the past continues to exist in the present.

For example: The light we see coming from the sun left the sun about $8\frac{1}{4}$ minutes ago. Light that we see coming from the star Antares left the star some 250 years ago. **(See fig. 71.)**

The newspaper sometimes reports that a nova (exploding star) has just occurred, but actually it took place in the past. It does take time for light to reach us, even though it travels at 186,000 miles per second.

It is theorized that if we were living in some other part of the universe, and if we had the right technical and astronomical equipment for viewing life on planet Earth, we could see what happened in the past. Depending on how many light years away we were from Earth, we would

Figure 71. LOOKING INTO THE PAST

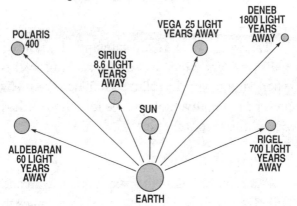

be able to witness momentous events of the past
as the light by which each event was made
visible, arrived where we happened to be. For
example, when the cameras on the Voyager
space probe took photographs of the planets
Jupiter, Saturn, Uranus, Neptune and Pluto, they
were transmitted via light waves back to planet
Earth. Traveling at the speed of light it took more
than an hour before the signals reached Earth
where they were converted into visible images
by technical apparatus for viewing. Thus each
image or picture was a picture of what happened
in the past. Depending on what part of the universe we happen to be in, such events as
Columbus' discovery of America, or even the
day Christ was crucified at Calvary, might just
now be arriving.

Looking into the Past.

If one were instantly transported to the star Sirius, with the right equipment, one would be able to see what he was doing nine years ago. In fact, one could watch what he had done for the last nine years.

We think video cameras are a fantastic invention. But they only record what happened at a particular time. What is truly amazing is that everything that everyone has done in the past is travelling via light rays through the universe. Jesus pointed out,

> For there is nothing hidden that will not be disclosed, and nothing concealed that will not be known or brought out into the open (Lk. 8:17).

Not only has God seen everything that has happened in the past, but He can still see it right now someplace in the universe. The light in which every act was committed is still traveling through space.

One might think that if he sinned at night or in a house then that would keep it from being exposed. But light is comprised of far more than just the light we see with our eyes. Light encompasses the entire magnetic spectrum — X-rays, TV and radio waves, radar, sonar, infrared, gamma, and ultraviolet waves. These all expose the physical world in one way or another, whether things are visible to the eye or not.

Covered by the Blood of the Lamb.

The bottom line is everything you have ever done is still being done throughout the universe — unless it has been covered by the blood of the Lamb. It is at this point that God "throws our sin in the sea of forgetfulness," which means He will not hold the sin nor the penalty of the sin against us.

This can only happen if there has been true repentance, a turning from sin, and a making of Christ the Lord and Savior of our lives.

> I, even I, am the one who wipes out
> your transgressions for My own sake;
> And I will not remember your sins
> (Isa. 43:25).

Part VI

THE END OF TIME AND THE COMING OF THE BIG BANG

Chapter Thirty

Another Whale of a Tale

The Rise of the Big Bang.

During the 1940s, the evolutionary idea arose that the universe was formed as the result of a huge explosion. From this explosion supposedly came, unaided, the entire universe — including galaxies, our sun, moon, the Earth and other planets, and the "goo" that produced you and everything else that lives in the zoo. This idea has been popularized as the "big bang" theory. **(See fig. 72.)**

According to this theory, life began as a tiny dot in space, and since the explosion, it is now speeding away from us and everything else in space. This, say astronomers, is confirmed by what is termed the "red shifting" (or Doppler Shift). This means the color of the light from distant stars and galaxies, when allowed to pass through a glass prism, is shifted toward the red end of the spectrum. A spectrum is created by

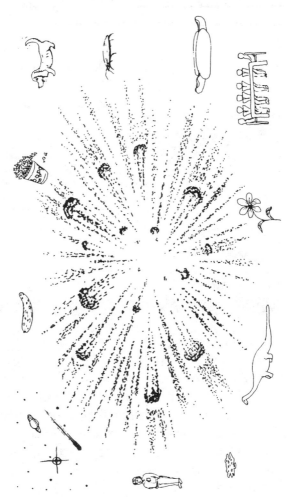

Figure 72. THE BIG BONER THEORY

Figure 73. THE MESSAGE OF THE STARS

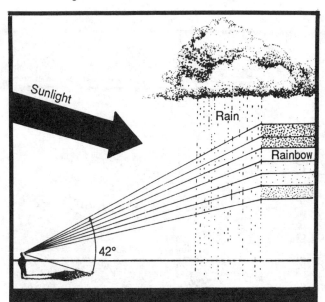

simply separating light into its bands of color —
like that of a rainbow, which occurs when light
coming from the sun passes through water drop-
lets suspended in the air. (**See fig. 73.**)

The term "red shifting" is an astronomical
expression which can be simply explained. If a
star is stationary in relation to us, its light waves
will reach us at a certain rate of speed and the
light will appear a certain color. If, however, the
star is moving away from us, fewer light waves

Figure 73. THE MESSAGE OF THE STARS (cont.)

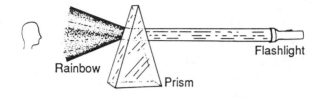

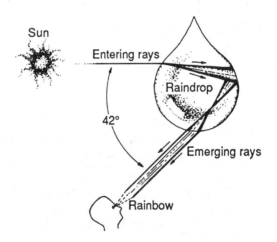

will reach us in a given time, and the light will
be shifted toward the red end of the spectrum. In
other words, it will be reddish in color. If the star
is moving toward us, the Doppler shift will be
toward the blue end of the spectrum and the star
will appear to be bluish. **(See fig. 74.)**

Figure 74. STRETCHING LIGHT WAVES

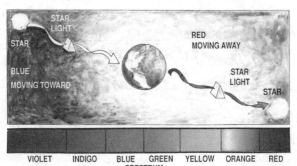

VIOLET	INDIGO	BLUE	GREEN	YELLOW	ORANGE	RED
			SPECTRUM			

This principle may be explained this way: A vehicle is approaching, and the driver is blowing his horn. The sound of the car's horn will continue to rise in pitch and volume as the car approaches. Once it passes, the sound waves take longer (stretched) to get to one's ear. As a result, the horn's pitch quickly drops until it becomes too faint to hear. **(See fig. 75.)** The longer it takes light from stars to get to us, the more red the light will appear in the spectrum. The shorter the period of time it takes to get to us, the more blue it will appear.

All stars and galaxies that are a great distance from us show a red shift. Evolutionary astronomers have assumed that this means that they are speeding away from us and that the farthest ones are traveling fastest. The inferences drawn from this are that the entire universe is expanding. One

Figure 75. STRETCHING SOUND WAVES

can see how evolutionists would assume that because of the "red shift" everything must be speeding away; and, therefore, if we tracked the galaxies backward, they came from a central point in an initial "big bang" explosion some 15-20 billion years ago.

This then is the evolutionary basis for the big bang theory. It has held sway over the evolutionary community since the 1960s, but has been experiencing a slow and gradual death as a result of new discoveries in the field of astronomy over the last several decades. These new discoveries reveal that there are just too many contradictions for the theory to be valid. Even so, it is still being taught as though it were a proven fact.

Scientific theories are always changing. A theory that may fit with the few facts known in the present may be replaced by a totally different and new theory which seems to fit the newly discovered data. Theologians who have attempted to make God's Word fit into the latest scientific dogma will once again have to adopt a new view.

Why not allow God's Word to stand on its own! The big bang notion is very different from what God has revealed in His Word regarding the origin of all things. It doesn't coincide with the order of events in Genesis One. Furthermore, it is purely a naturalistic, mechanistic explanation of how the universe made itself and excludes any supernatural involvement whatsoever.

To refuse to believe God's Word and prefer such a ridiculous theory is the epitome of pride. Pride is the characteristic found in Satan. It led to the original "big bang" when Satan, in a flash, was cast from God's presence. Maybe the reason that caricatures of Satan are always red is because of the red shift. Since the direction of his exit from God's throne was outward, the color of this angel of light is apparently toward the red end of the spectrum. Of course, this is only speculation, but it may explain why Satan is most always pictured in red.

Chapter Thirty-One

The Death of the Big Bang

A short time ago, a flurry of newspaper articles and TV news clips appeared proclaiming that the big bang theory had finally been proven. It all began when the satellite COBE sent back information which caused one astronomer to ignorantly announce: "It was like looking at God, if you're religious." The secular media went wild after this news broke. Almost all the articles mentioned God, but in a derogatory way, many suggesting the "big bang" itself was God.

Enthusiasm was sparked because for years the big bang theory has been near death's door within the scientific community. Many discoveries in recent years have extremely weakened the theory. One recent astronomical discovery reveals a major inconsistency: The universe is "lumpy" (kind of like lumpy oatmeal), rather than smooth. This "lumpiness," as it is called,

Figure 76. THE ORIGIN OF THE BIG BONER THEORY

refers to the huge clusters of millions of galaxies all clumped together with great voids in between.

The big bang explosion should have produced an *even* distribution of all matter and energy in all directions. However, this is not the case. This discrepancy led evolutionary astronomers to propose that there must have been a "lumpiness" in the original big bang explosion. Even though the laws of physics regarding explosions do not allow for such, evolutionists were determined to find evidence to support this "lumpiness."

The search supposedly ended when the satelite COBE sent back radiation data which was said to have recorded the leftover "whisper" or "echo" of low-level radiation (heat) from the supposedly original big bang explosion. In this "whisper" there was said to be a record of small fluctuations (lumpiness) of radiation heat that was 30 millionths of a degree. Presumptuously, they declared the big bang now a "proven" fact. God was no longer in the picture at all.

However, according to one of the designers of the COBE satellite, although it carried a very sophisticated package of equipment for research into the workings of the universe, it was not capable of measuring fluctuations as minute as

30 millionths of a degree. This is confirmed in the *Science Journal* of May 1, 1992 (pg. 612).

It is amazing the extremes that a scientist will go to in order to remain "king." He will do anything to try to disprove the idea of any other King of the universe. Whether the big bang happened or not is really not the issue at all. The issue still is and always will be the existence of God. Can He exist? For the evolutionist, He must not exist. Nevertheless, the big bang has not been "saved" from death's door but has had a temporary reprieve; judgment will come at some future date.

What appears to be bogus evolutionary perception regarding the big bang and the origin of the universe may, in fact, contain an element of truth. It may be that the big bang is yet to come, as we shall see.

Chapter Thirty-Two

Swallowed by a Black Hole

Black Holes.

Many skeptics, both past and present, have ridiculed the account of Jonah's being swallowed by a whale. Yet today there is a whale of a tale being told by the scientific community about something in the heavens that may be swallowing the entire universe. Though evolutionary scientists can't conceive of a whale swallowing Jonah, they claim a black hole is swallowing the universe.

Some astronomers theorize that black holes may be drawing in and absorbing other celestial bodies. If this is true, the entire universe may slowly be being drawn into these "death stars." Sounds like fantasy, but there may be just as much truth to this tale as there is to Jonah's account. Just as Jonah's "light" was sucked into

Figure 77. GAS GUZZLERS

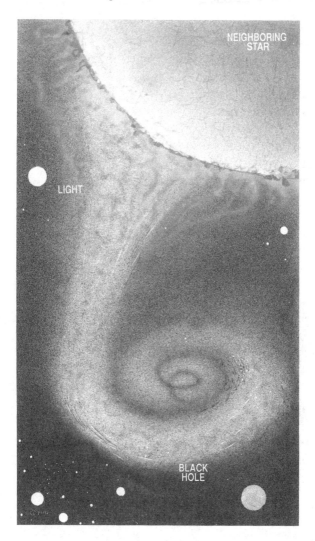

the dark pit inside a whale, so the light of the entire universe may be being swallowed into an abyss.

Astronomers believe that at the end of a star's life it totally collapses and ends up becoming a black hole — the most powerful energy force known to man. The star's powerful gravity has overcome everything else, crushing its own matter into a volume so small that it virtually ceases to exist. Though all external evidence of its presence disappears, the star leaves behind a tremendous force of gravity. Anything that falls into it is crushed out of existence. It is believed that black holes can compress the mass of a million stars into a volume smaller than that of an atom. Some black holes have such a strong gravitational pull that the light coming from nearby stars sags or is pulled into them; normally light is hardly affected by gravity. The black hole sucks in anything and everything that comes within a certain distance; it is a bottomless pit from which there is no escape. Its power can bend light and it attracts light like a magnet attracts metal.

This powerful physical phenomenon may illustrate hell. Luke 16 describes hell as "an impassable gulf."

> And besides all this, between us and you a great chasm has been fixed, so

that those who want to go from here to you cannot, nor can anyone cross over from there to us (Lk. 16:26).

Hell, of course, is reserved for Satan, his demons and all those who have chosen to follow him. To be sentenced to hell one must have rejected the Creator God and His way of escape, Jesus Christ.

Back to Barry.

Barry Setterfield's research on the speed of light as covered in Chapter 10 has led to some additional staggering revelations. Setterfield has shown how the entire universe could in fact be disappearing into a huge black hole. He has suggested an alternative to the big bang theory. His calculations indicate that the universe is contracting, not expanding. A contracting universe should show a blue shift, not a red one. So how is it that there is a red shift in the light coming from distant stars?

There are various ways in which light coming from distant stars may be shifted to the red side of the spectrum. A red shift can be produced by a slowing light speed. The decay of the speed of light was covered in Chapter 10. A red shift from a declining light speed can more than counter the blue shift. It overrides, so to speak, the blue shift.

Another way in which the color of light coming from distant stars can be reddened is by gravity fields and dust, both of which are plentiful in space. Exceptionally red sunsets or sunrises appear so because of dust or moisture in the atmosphere. So it is possible that the so-called "red shift" may be a result of gravity, dust, a combination of these or even something else.

Setterfield feels that the contraction is so great that the universe itself may actually be a black hole. If so, as the universe collapses, it will eventually destroy itself. Setterfield has not yet completed the calculations to determine when that would occur.

Chapter Thirty-Three

The Coming of the Big Bang

The evolutionary notion of the universe evolving as a result of a big bang in which a tiny cosmic egg smaller than the size of an atom exploded is nothing more than 20th-century mythology. The idea of a big bang coming soon to the universe may be closer to the truth.

It is a well-known fact that stars are dying. They are experiencing what is called the nova effect. When a star comes to the end of its life, it goes through a process of death in which it uses up the fuel that causes it to burn.

The question from a creation science standpoint is: How is it possible for a star to burn up in just a few thousand years if the universe is only several thousand years old?

The solution involves the speed of light at the beginning of creation as we discussed earlier. Not only was the speed of light much greater at the beginning of creation, but stars were experi-

Figure 78. THE COMING OF THE BIG BANG

encing nuclear reactions so fast that they burned much more fuel going through an entire life cycle and exploding, releasing fantastic amounts of light and energy. The amount of fuel they burned in a matter of hours was equal to that which, at the present rate, would take several billion years.

Is this feasible or is this just another Star Wars episode? Right now there are quasars — stars said to be on the edge of the universe — that are the size of a normal star and yet give off as much light as an entire galaxy (100 billion stars). No known reactions of any kind could supply the tremendous amount of energy they expend.

The speed of light on creation day was so great that light from an exploding star was able to travel the thousands of light years from the center of our galaxy to the Earth in just a couple of seconds. Since the curse, the speed of light — as well as the nuclear reactions — have no doubt been slowing down so that stars don't burn out as quickly. What appear to be older stars are really only stars that are hours or a few days older than what is known as young stars.

Blinking Stars.

If the speed of light is constant, then we should be seeing stars blinking on as well as blinking off (burning out). Suppose one lives on the side of a mountain overlooking a small town in the valley. During the evenings, the lights from the town are visible. As time passes, additional lights appear and one knows that there are new homes and businesses being built. On the other hand, if one never saw lights being added to the town but instead noticed that the number of lights were diminishing, he would have to conclude that the town was probably dwindling in population.

Likewise, if the universe is billions of years old, the light from some of the remote stars should be suddenly appearing in the night sky, their light just now reaching our planet. But this is not the case. We see stars only blinking out, not on. This tells us that the big bang theory is really the "big boner" theory. The universe is not the result of a giant explosion, with stars forming throughout time. Rather it is the result of creation; and because of the curse, the law of decay known as the Second Law of Thermodynamics is resulting in the burning out of stars. In time, the whole universe will collapse.

The Future of the Universe.

> Jesus said, "Immediately after the tribulation of those days shall the sun be darkened" (Matt. 24:29 KJV).

The apostle John was shown an apocalyptic

vision of the world during the last days of the great tribulation, and he wrote that because of the sun, "Men were scorched with great heat" (Rev. 16:9 KJV).

> The prophet Isaiah wrote of this time, "The light of the sun shall be sevenfold, as the light of seven days" (Isa. 30:26).

> The prophet Joel predicted that when the great and terrible day of the Lord would come, "The sun shall be turned into darkness" (Joel 2:31 KJV).

Our Sun's End.

For many years astronomers concluded that our sun could maintain its present heat-energy output for at least 5 billion more years because its hydrogen supply was only about half exhausted. However, more recently, astronomers have reappraised this theory. Now many believe that once a star (our sun is a medium-sized star) has expended half its hydrogen, it is in danger of experiencing a nova. Larger stars supernova (blow up). Smaller stars, like our own sun, nova — get brighter and hotter for 7 to 14 days, then become darker. There are about a dozen novas a year in the observable universe. **(See fig. 79.)**

Figure 79. THE NOVA OF OUR SUN

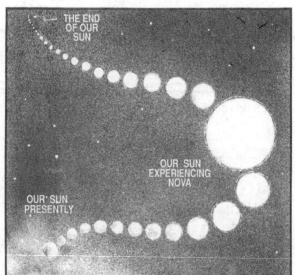

Some astronomers now believe that the increased sun-spot activity on our own sun is a sign that it may be about to nova. The nova of our sun would most assuredly:

1. Cause the sun to become unusually bright as Isaiah prophesied.
2. Become seven times hotter as John prophesied.
3. And then become dark as Joel and Jesus prophesied.

"Lift Up Your Eyes...."

In light of the above, the following passages from the Bible take on new meaning:

> Lift up your eyes to the heavens, look at the Earth beneath; the heavens will vanish like smoke, the Earth will wear out like a garment and its inhabitants die like flies. But my salvation will last forever, my righteousness will never fail (Isa. 51:6).

> But the day of the Lord will come like a thief. The heavens will disappear with a roar; the elements will be destroyed by fire, and the Earth and everything in it will be laid bare (II Pet. 3:10 NIV).

> I watched as he opened the sixth seal. There was a great earthquake. The sun turned black like sackcloth made of goat hair, the whole moon turned blood red and the stars in the sky fell to Earth, as late figs drop from a fig tree when shaken by a strong wind. The sky receded like a scroll, rolling

up, and every mountain and island was removed from its place (Rev. 6:12-14).

The Big Bang is Coming!

Evolutionism assumes that the universe began with a big bang. However, it appears that evolutionism has the story in reverse. Scripture has the "big bang" coming at the close of time rather than at the beginning.

The powerful forces such as seen in the heavens are but some of the sources available to God to bring about the final judgment and His plan of the ages for mankind. They reveal His power and control over His creation.

The heavens are displaying the glory of God (Psa. 19:1).

Chapter Thirty-Four

The End of Time and the Beginning of a New Age

Soon, very soon, the present age will come to a close and the new age, which will last forever, will be ushered into existence. The day is coming when time as we know it will be no more. Instead, the Father of Time will take His place. His Name is Jesus, and He will be the source of time. He will determine the timing of all future events. Such events will not be ruled by the hands of a 24-hour clock, but rather by the nail-scarred hands of the sacrificial Lamb of God. The yearly calendar will not be ruled by the solar sun, but rather by the only begotten Son (Rev. 22:5).

One of the first planned events on His calendar is the Wedding Supper.

> Then the angels said to me, Write:
> 'Blessed are those who are invited to

the wedding supper of the lamb!' (Rev.
19:9).

This marriage feast will be the most spectacular banquet the universe has ever known. It will
be prepared for the King of the Universe and His
Bride. The Groom and His bride will rule and
reign together throughout eternity. No one
knows for certain exactly how it will occur, but
the Bible gives us some clues.

The Coming Mystery.

Listen, I tell you a mystery: We will
not all sleep, but we will all be changed
(I Cor. 15:51).

Look, he is coming with the clouds,
and every eye will see him, even those
who pierced him; and all the peoples
of the earth will mourn because of
him. So shall it be! Amen (Rev. 1:7).

The Resurrection of the Dead.

In a flash, in the twinkling of an eye,
at the last trumpet. For the trumpet will
sound, the dead will be raised im-
perishable, and we will be changed (I
Cor. 15:52).

At that time the sign of the Son of Man will appear in the sky, and all the nations of the earth will mourn. They will see the Son of Man coming on the clouds of the sky, with power and great glory (Matt. 24:30).

The Return of the Messiah.

For the Lord himself will come down from heaven, with a loud command, with the voice of the archangel and with the trumpet call of God, and the dead in Christ will rise first (I Thes. 4:16). **(See fig. 80.)**

The Heavens will Disappear.

But the day of the Lord will come like a thief. The heavens will disappear with a roar; the elements will be destroyed by fire, and the earth and everything in it will be laid bare (II Pet. 3:10).

By the same word the present heavens and earth are reserved for fire, being kept for the day of judgment and destruction of ungodly men (II Pet. 3:7).

Figure 80. THE RETURN OF JESUS

As you look forward to the day of God and speed its coming. That day will bring about the destruction of the heavens by fire, and the elements will melt in the heat (II Pet. 3:12).

This will happen when the Lord Jesus is revealed from heaven in blazing fire with his powerful angels (II Thes. 1:7,8).

Creation of a New Heavens.

Then I saw a new heaven and a new earth, for the first heaven and the first earth had passed away, and there was no longer any sea (Rev. 21:1).

No More Sun.

There will be no more night. They will not need the light of a lamp or the light of the sun, for the Lord God will give them light. And they will reign for ever and ever (Rev. 22:5).

Then the King will say to those on his right, 'Come, you who are blessed by my Father; take your inheritance, the kingdom prepared for you since the creation of the world' (Matt. 25:34).

Eternal Punishment for the Wicked.

Then they will go away to eternal punishment, but the righteous to eternal life (Matt. 25:46).

Hope for the Repentant.

Praise be to the God and Father of our Lord Jesus Christ! In his great mercy he has given us new birth into a living hope through the resurrection of Jesus Christ from the dead (I Pet. 1:3).

And into an inheritance that can never perish, spoil or fade—kept in heaven for you (I Pet. 1:4).

To him who overcomes, I will give the right to sit with me on my throne, just as I overcame and sat down with my Father on his throne (Rev. 3:21).

The Righteous Will Live Forever.

There will be no more night. They will

not need the light of a lamp or the light of the sun, for the Lord God will give them light. And they will reign for ever and ever (Rev. 22:5).

COME QUICKLY, LORD JESUS!

BIBLIOGRAPHY

Ackerman, Paul D. *It's a Young World After All*. Grand Rapids, MI: Baker Book House, 1986.

Barnes, Thomas G. *Origin and Destiny of Earth's Magnetic Field*. El Cajon, CA: Institute for Creation Research, 1973.

Becklake, Sue. *Space, Stars, Planets and Spacecraft*. New York, NY: Dorling Kindersley, 1991.

Gentry, Robert V. *Creation's Tiny Mystery*. Knoxville, TN: Earth Science Associates, 1986.

Gramfors, Bo. *Earth Facts*. Denver, CO: Earthbooks, Inc., 1990.

Ham, Ken, Andrew Snelling and Carl Wieland. *The Answers Book*. El Cajon, CA: Master Books, 1990.

Heinze, Thomas F. *Creation vs. Evolution Handbook*. Grand Rapids, MI: Baker Book House, 1973.

Hill, Harold with Irene Harrel. *From Goo to You by Way of the Zoo*. Plainfield, NJ: Logos International, 1976.

Jackson, Wayne. *Creation, Evolution and Age of the Earth*. Stockton, CA: Courier Publications, 1989.

Kester, Phyllis with Dr. Monty Kester. *What's All This Monkey Business?* Harrison, AR: New Leaf Press, 1981.

Kofahl, Ph.D., Robert E. *Handy Dandy Evolution Refuter*. San Diego, CA: Beta Books, 1977.

McLean, Dr. G.S., Roger Oakland and Larry McLean. *The Evidence for Creation*. Saskatchewan, Canada: Full Gospel Bible Institute, 1989.

Mitton, Jacqueline and Simon. *Discovering Astronomy*. London, England: Trewin Copplestone Books, Ltd., 1979.

Morris, Henry M. *The Beginning of the World*. Denver, CO: Accent Books, 1977.

Morris, Henry M. *The Remarkable Birth of Planet Earth*. San Diego, CA: Institute for Creation Research, 1972.

Morris, Ph.D. Henry M., *Scientific Creationism*. San Diego, CA: Creation-Life Publishers, 1974.

Overn, William. *Creator's Signature*. Minneapolis, MN: Bible-Science Association, 1981.

Ozanne, C.G. *The First 7000 Years*. Jericho, New York: Exposition Press, Inc., 1970.

Petersen, Dennis R., *Unlocking the Mysteries of Creation*. South Lake Tahoe, CA: Christian Equippers International, 1986.

The Random House Encyclopedia (3rd Edition). New York, NY: Random House, Inc. 1990.

Rehwinkel, Alfred M. *The Age of the Earth and Chronology of the Bible*. Adelaide, South Australia: Lutheran Publishing House, 1966.

Rehwinkel, Alfred M. *The Wonders of Creation*. Grand Rapids, MI: Baker Book House, 1974.

Sharp, Douglas B. *The Revolution Against Evolution*. Lansing, MI: Mount Hope Int'l Outreach Center, 1986.

Slusher, Harold S. and Thomas Gamwell. *Age of*

the Earth. El Cajon, CA: Institute for Creation Science, 1978.

Slusher, Harold S. *Age of the Cosmos*. San Diego, CA: Institute for Creation Research, 1980.

Slusher, Harold S. and Stephen J. Robertson. *Age of the Solar System*. El Cajon, CA: Institute for Creation Research, 1982.

Slusher, Harold S. *Critique of Radiometric Dating*. San Diego, CA: Institute for Creation Research, 1973.

Smith, A.E. Wilder. *The Natural Sciences Know Nothing of Evolution*. San Diego, CA: Master Books, 1981.

Time-Life Books. *Solar System*. Alexandria, VA. 1985.

Time-Life Books. *Space & Planets*. Alexandria, VA. 1992.

Whitcomb, John. *Early Earth*. Grand Rapids, MI: Baker Book House, 1986.

White, Dr. A.J. Monty. *How Old is the Earth?* Herts, England: Evangelical Press, 1985.

Wilson, Dr. Clifford. *Creation or Evolution: Facts or Fairytales*. Victoria, Australia: Pacific College, Inc., 1985.

LIST OF GRAPHS AND ILLUSTRATIONS